The Book Of Lost Verses
Book 1

Mark Humes

Artist Statement

My thoughts, feelings, and experiences make up the sum of who I am In every work of art that I create; I leave behind thoughts and feelings in captured visual representations as expressions of the human condition I experience. One work of art at a time I offer a piece of my soul to the world with hopes than in time, something of myself will live on in every patron of my art.

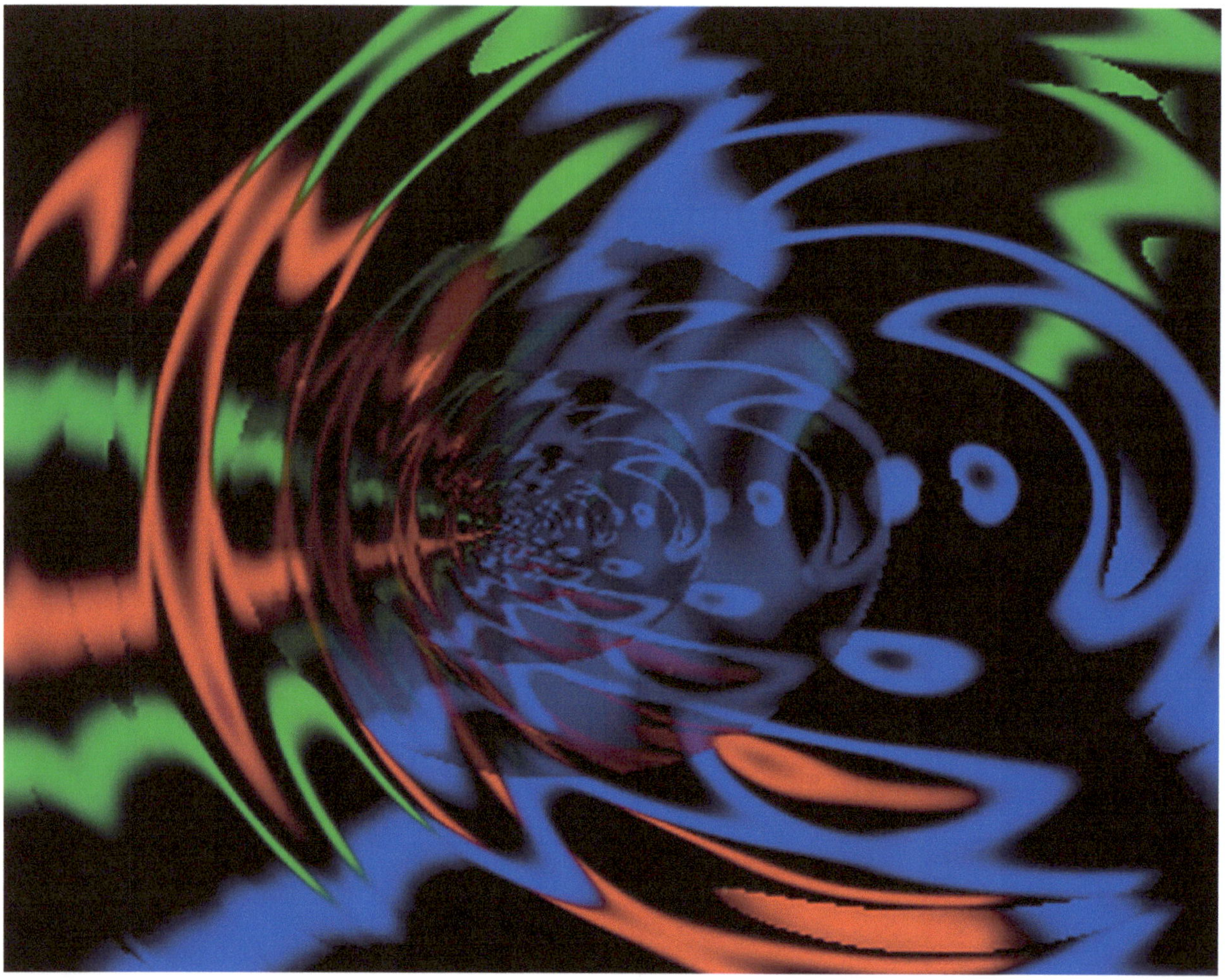

RACING DUALITY

Channeling the emotions of manic depression into a visual form.
My racing duality is finding order in chaos and choosing the beauty
of the chaotic

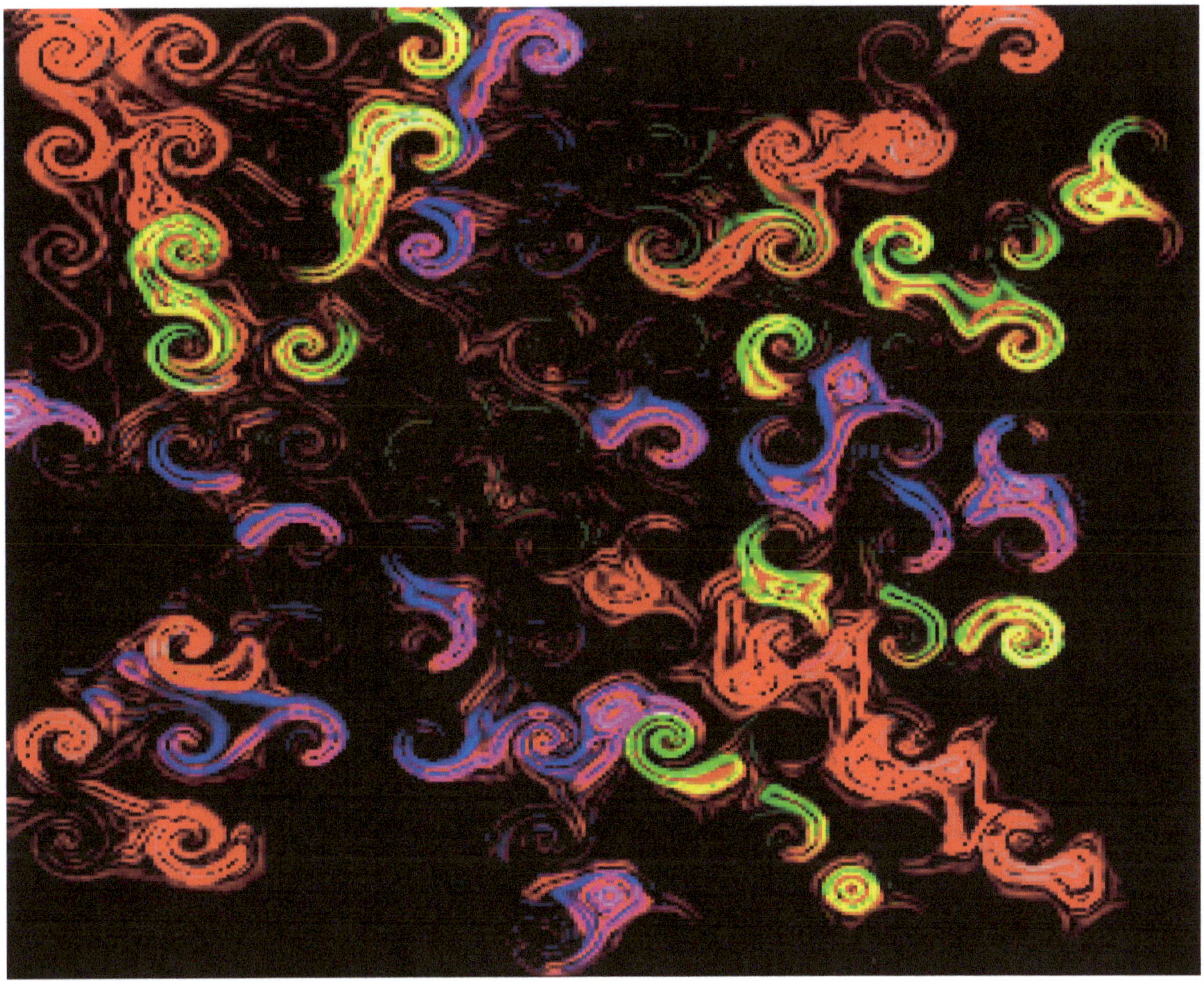

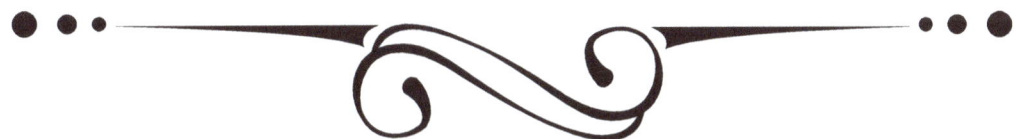

AMUSEMENT OF THE LOST

On many occasions, I found myself lost, and soon, amusement engulfed fear as the exploration of new horizons called to me from that same harrowing place of ignorance.

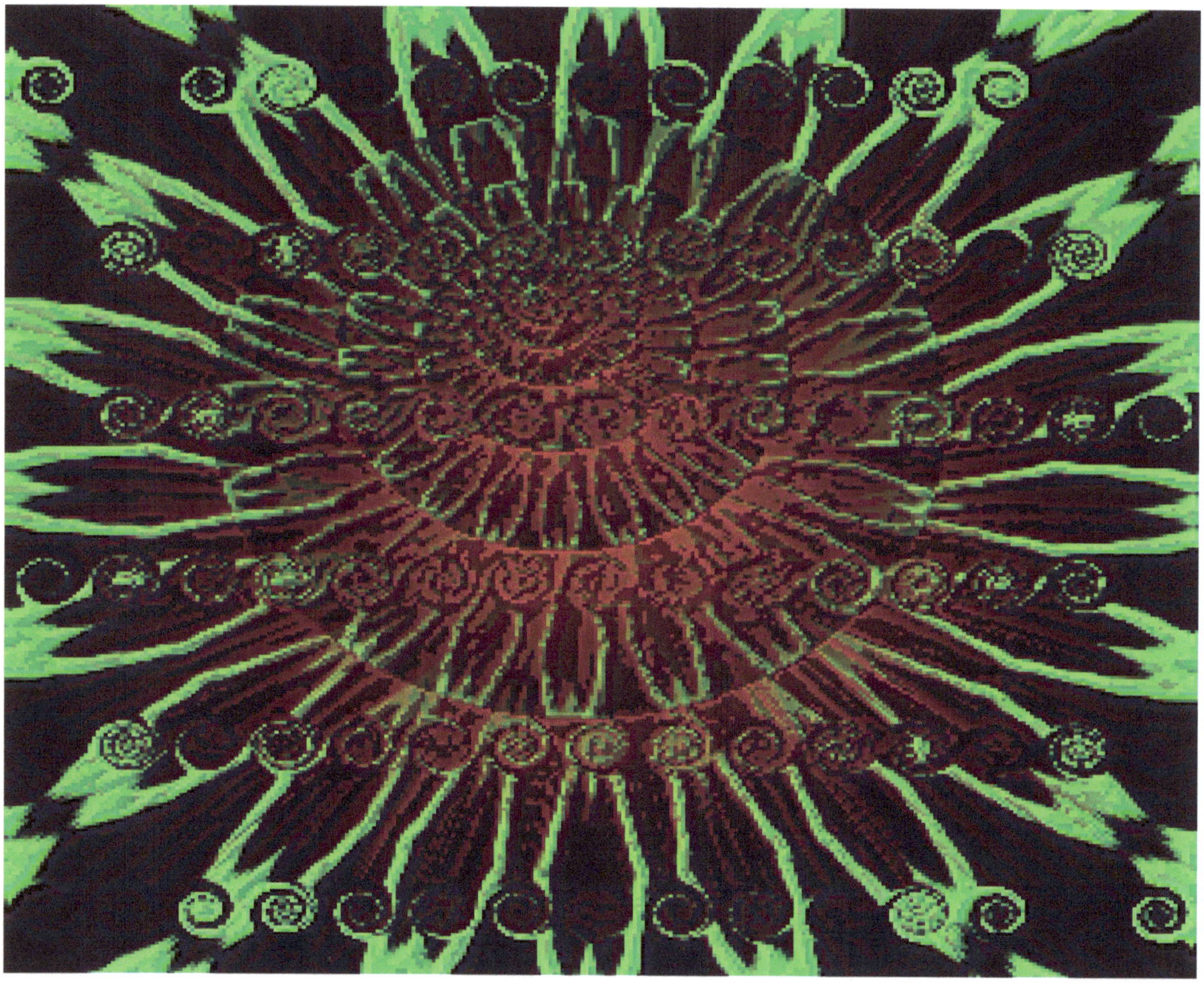

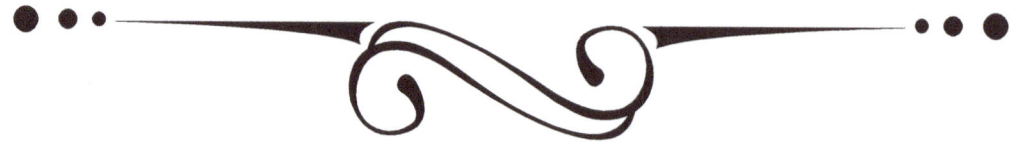

FROM WITHIN

Moments of anger channeled correctly will blossom into new realities and bring new opportunities into existence, and often all it takes is a scream from within to find the determination.

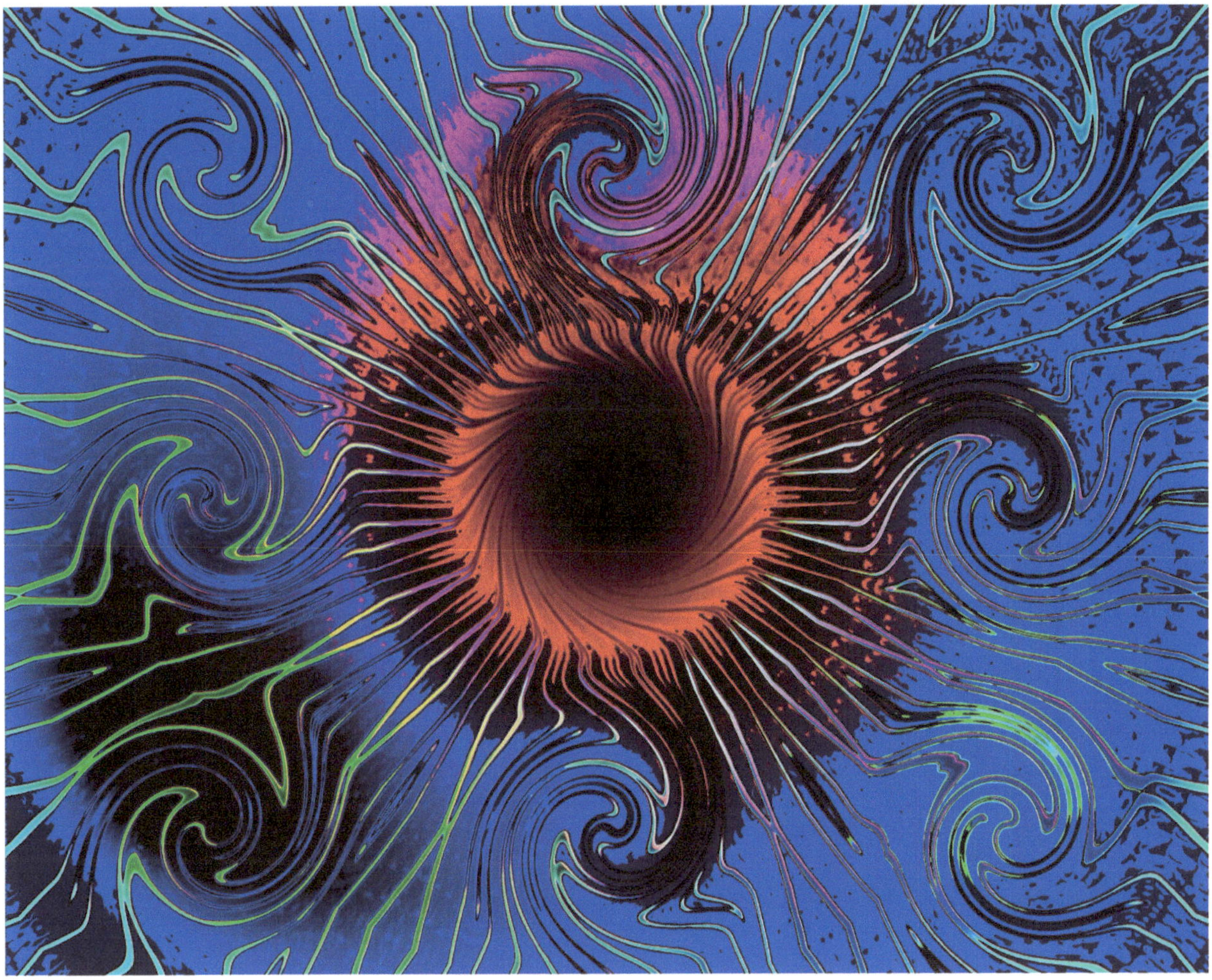

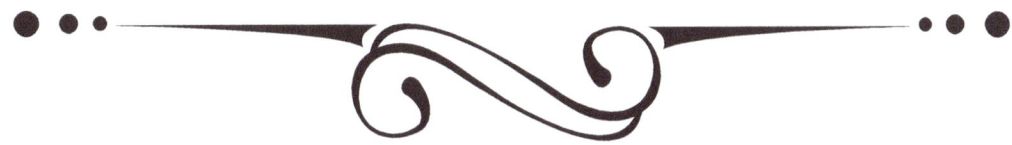

FEED THE HOLE

An empty heart will not endure. The echoing thought ripples through the mind feed the hole.

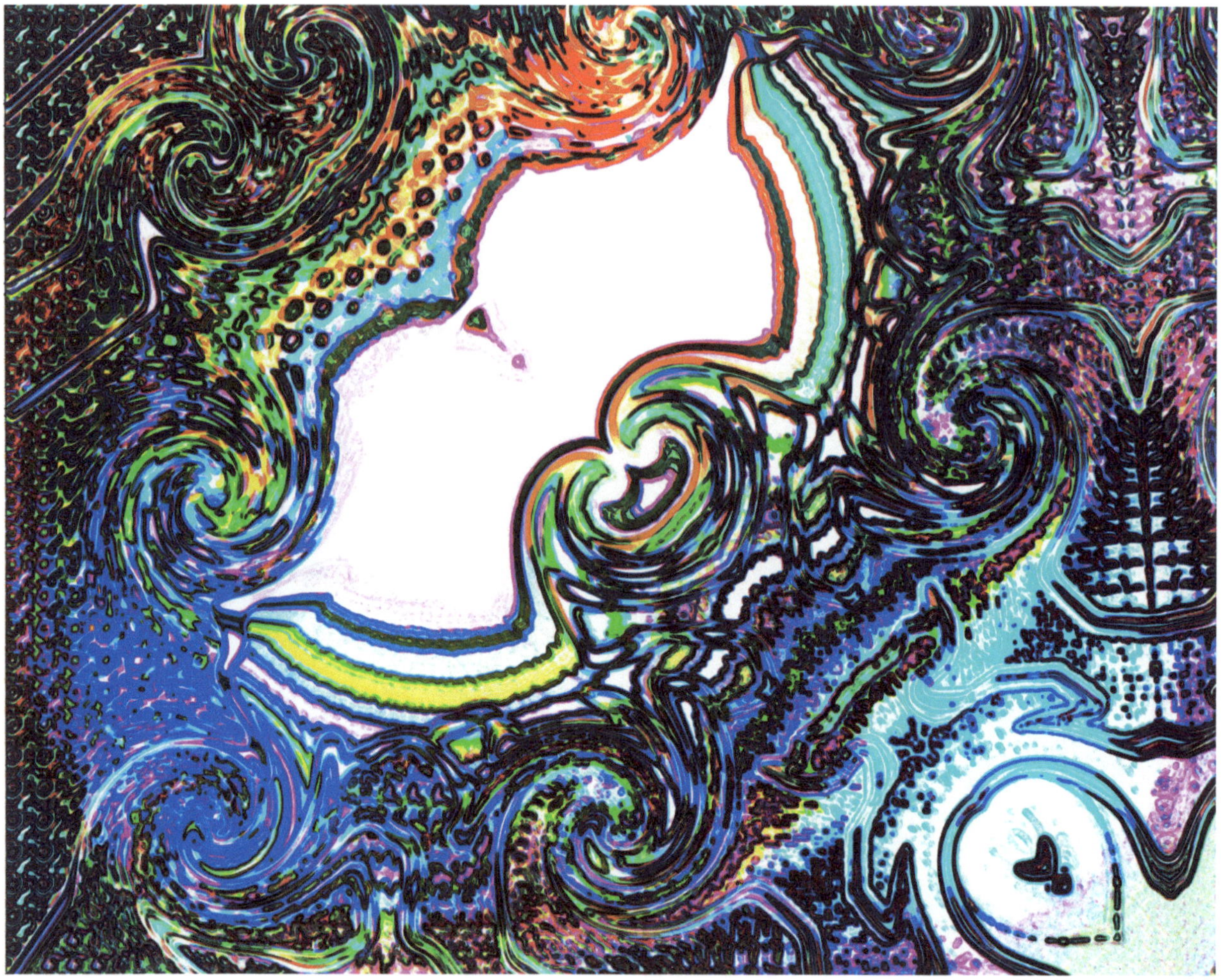

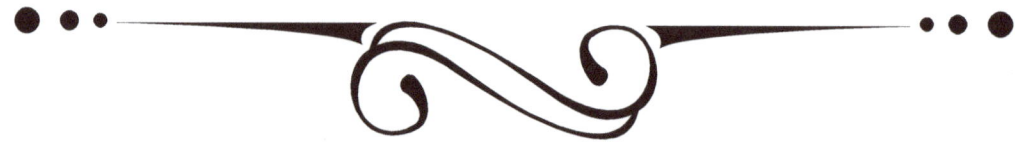

DOGU

The Dogu, Unexplained from ancient times passed. Visitors or just creatures of a different mind like my own. I have moments when I look at the world and would like to believe I am Dogu.

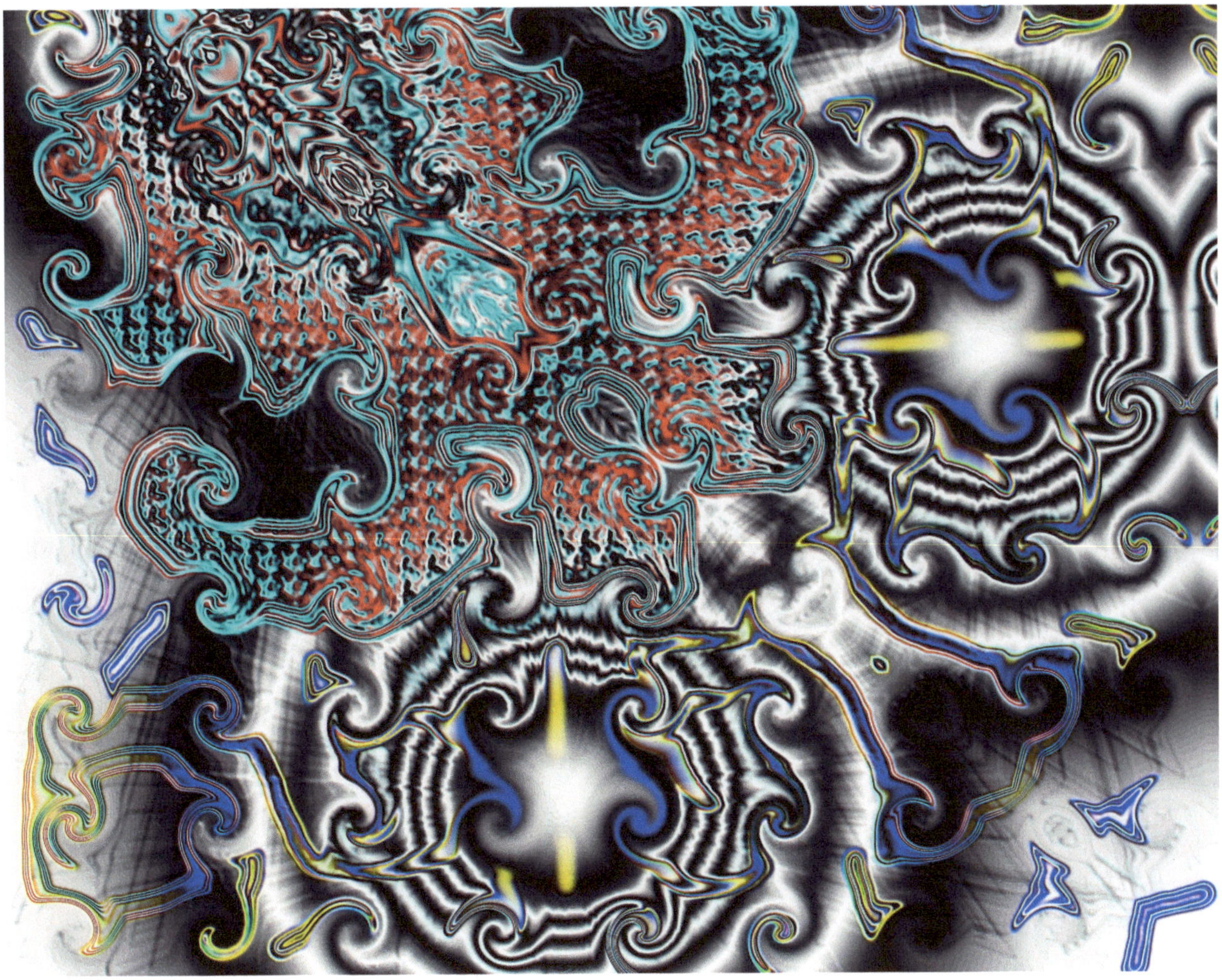

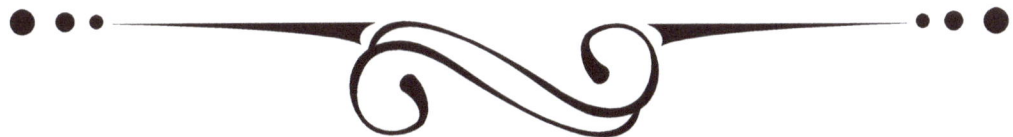

AMENONUHOKO

The spear of creation was passed down from the elders. This reminder is always humbling. Knowing that even the most powerful of us owe everything to those who came before us.

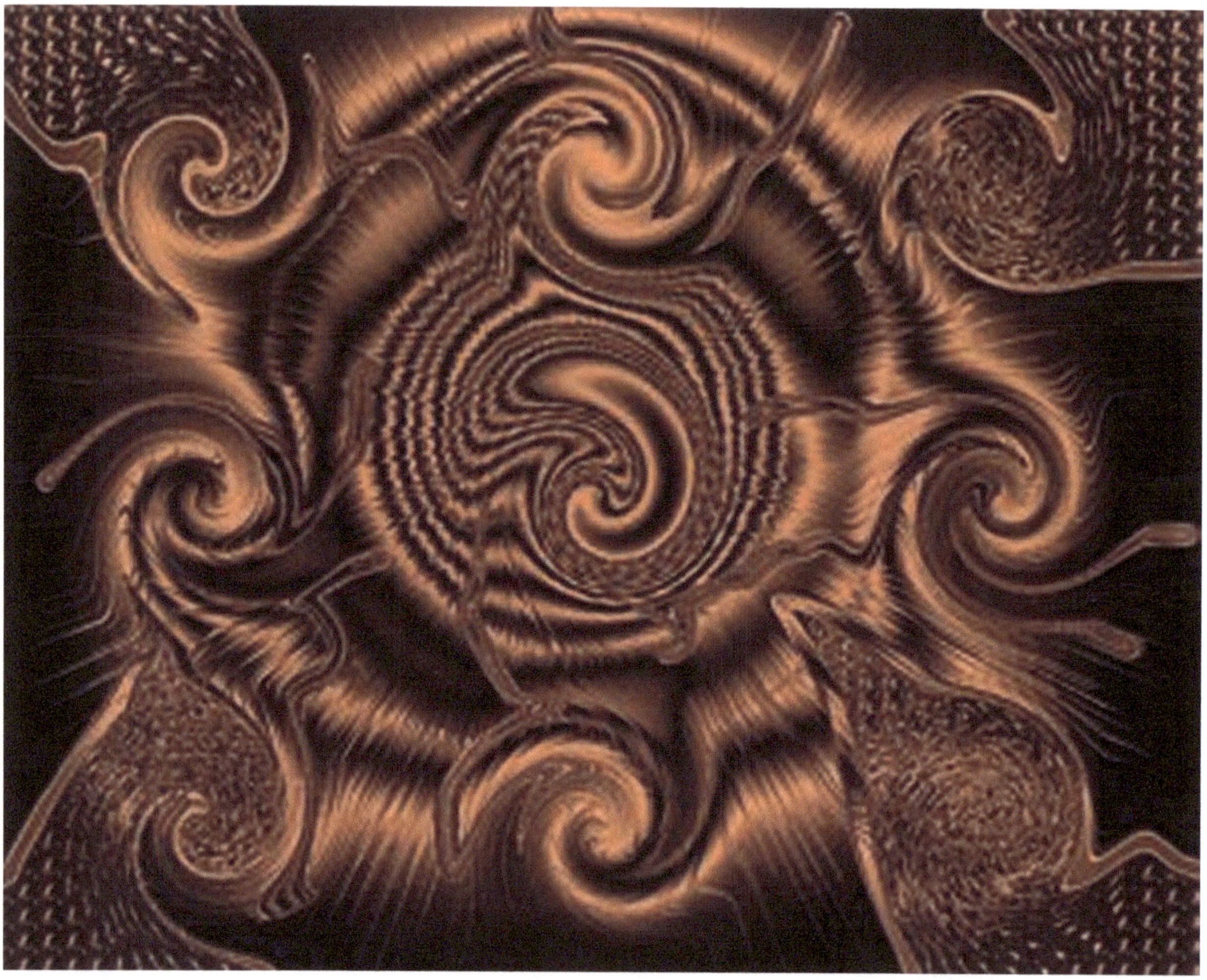

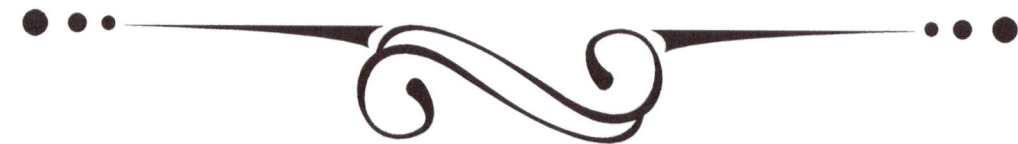

SOLAR IMPACT

I looked into the sun and saw power meet power and the ancient source of all life endure.

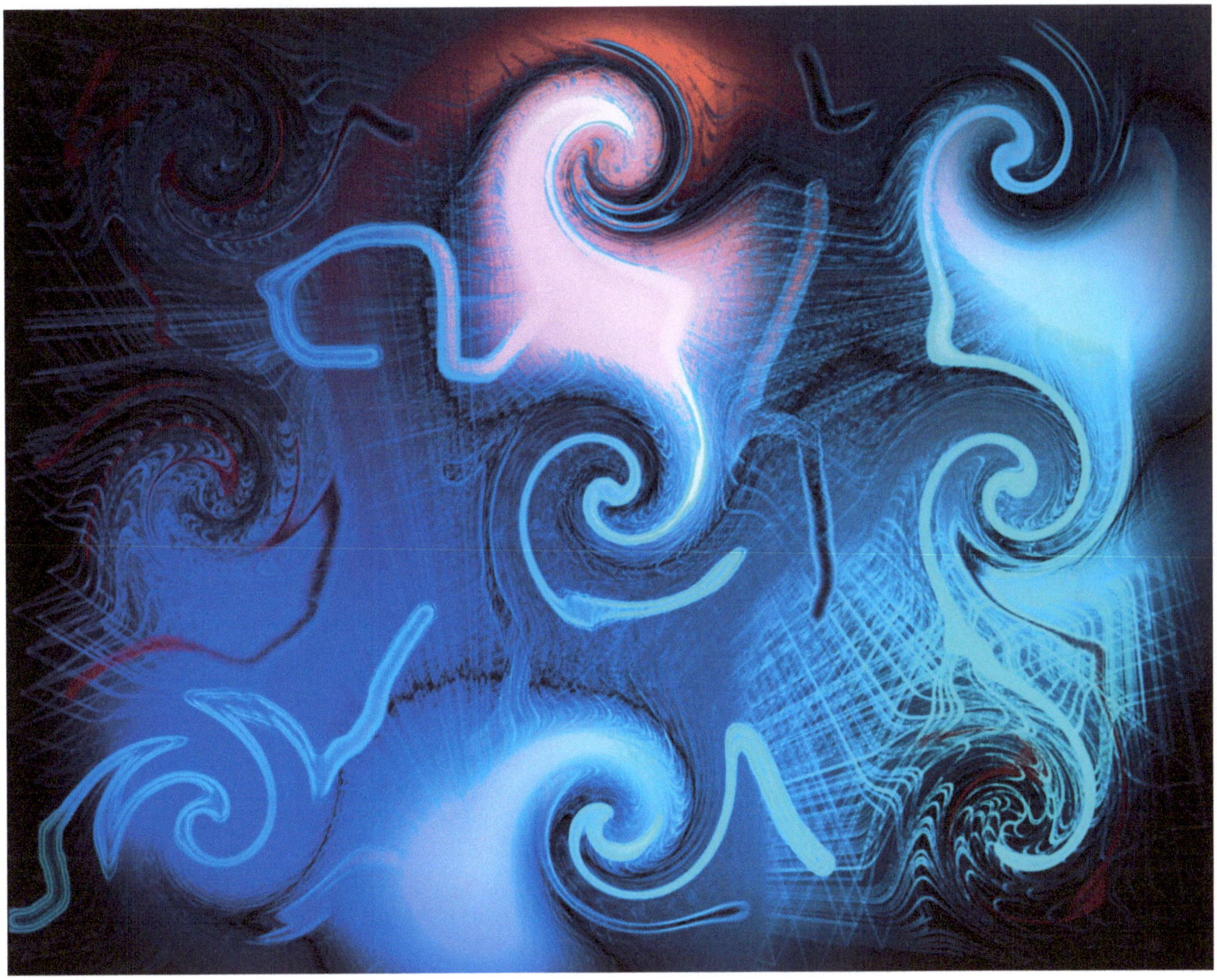

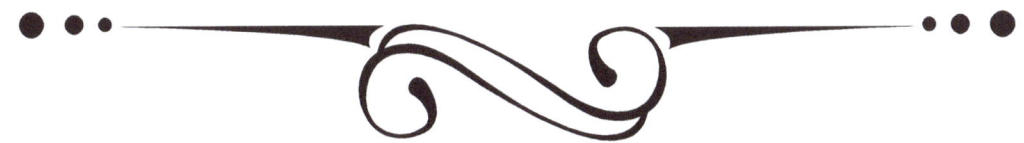

WHEN REALITY BREAKS

That moment when reality breaks and everything changes, you can see the cracks form. One small change in your perception and reality breaks.

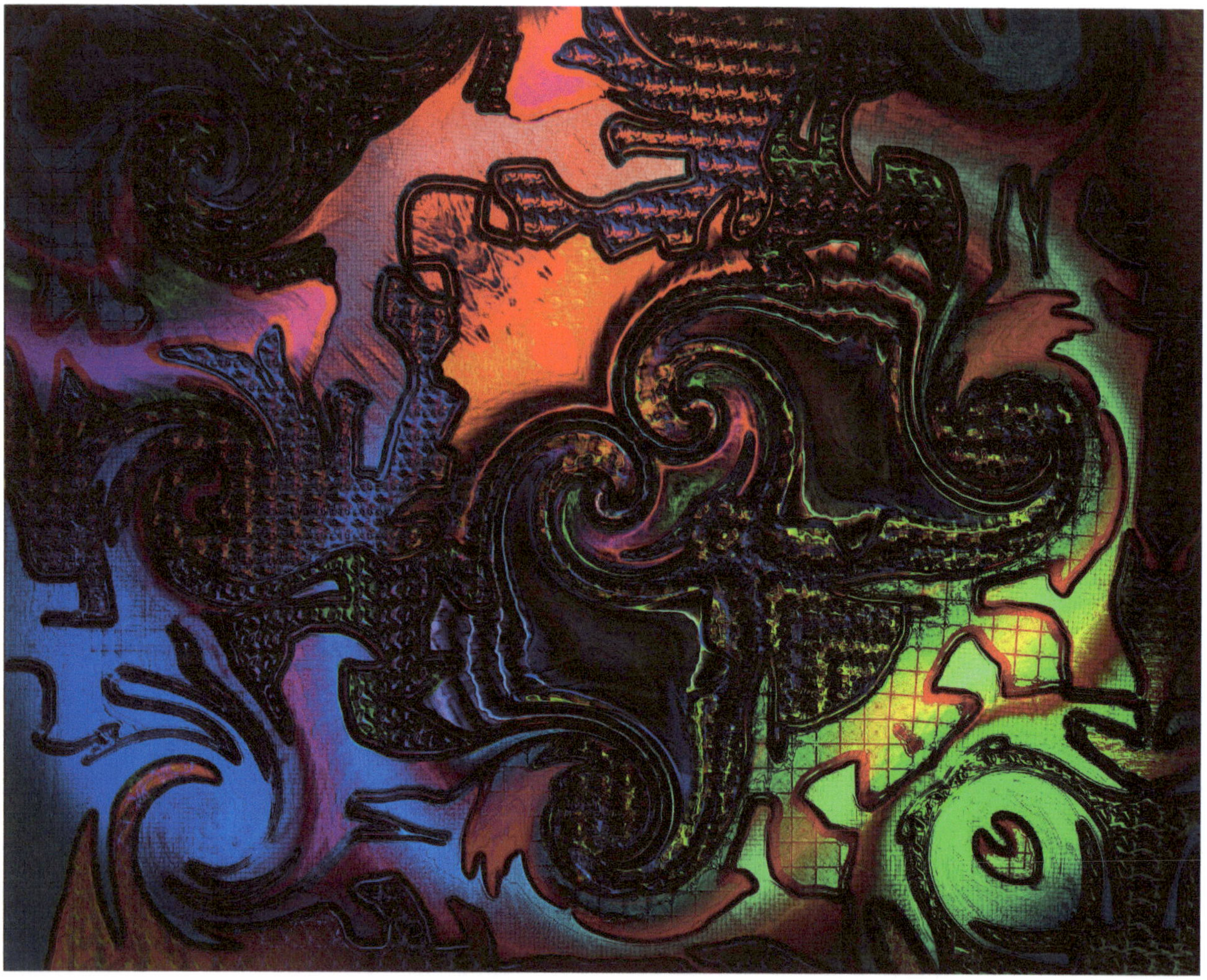

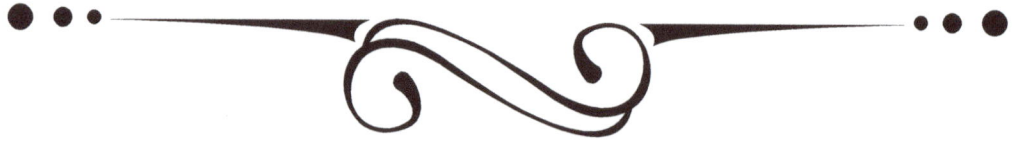

THE LAIR OF JÖRMUNGANDR

Deep in his jeweled lair in the abyss of the sea. Jörmungandr remains for the final battle. The feeling that we must be vigilant against our foes is a powerful inborn emotion that can overcome us at any time.

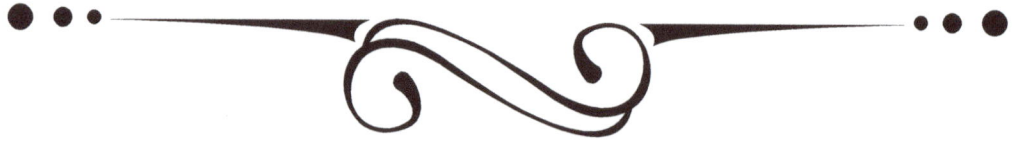

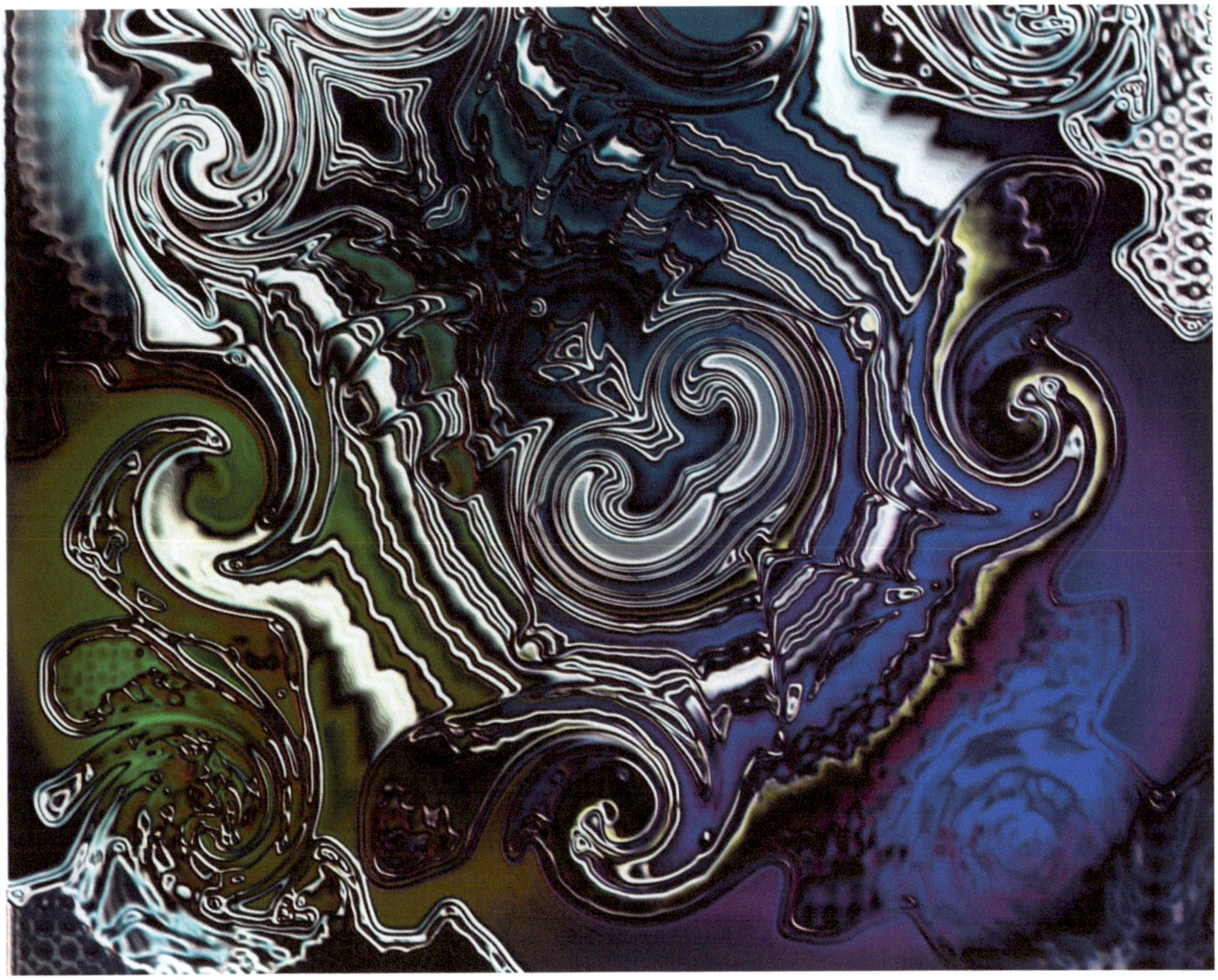

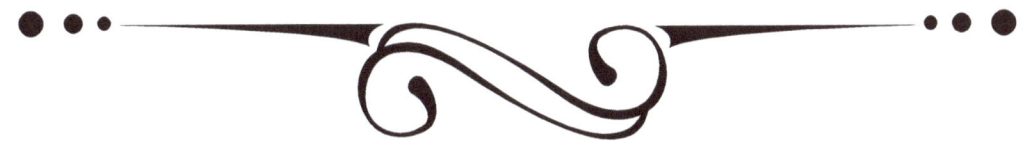

THE QUEEN OF THE NECROPOLIS

She guards the underworld breathing new life into old bones. The guardian of the end and the mother of the beginning.

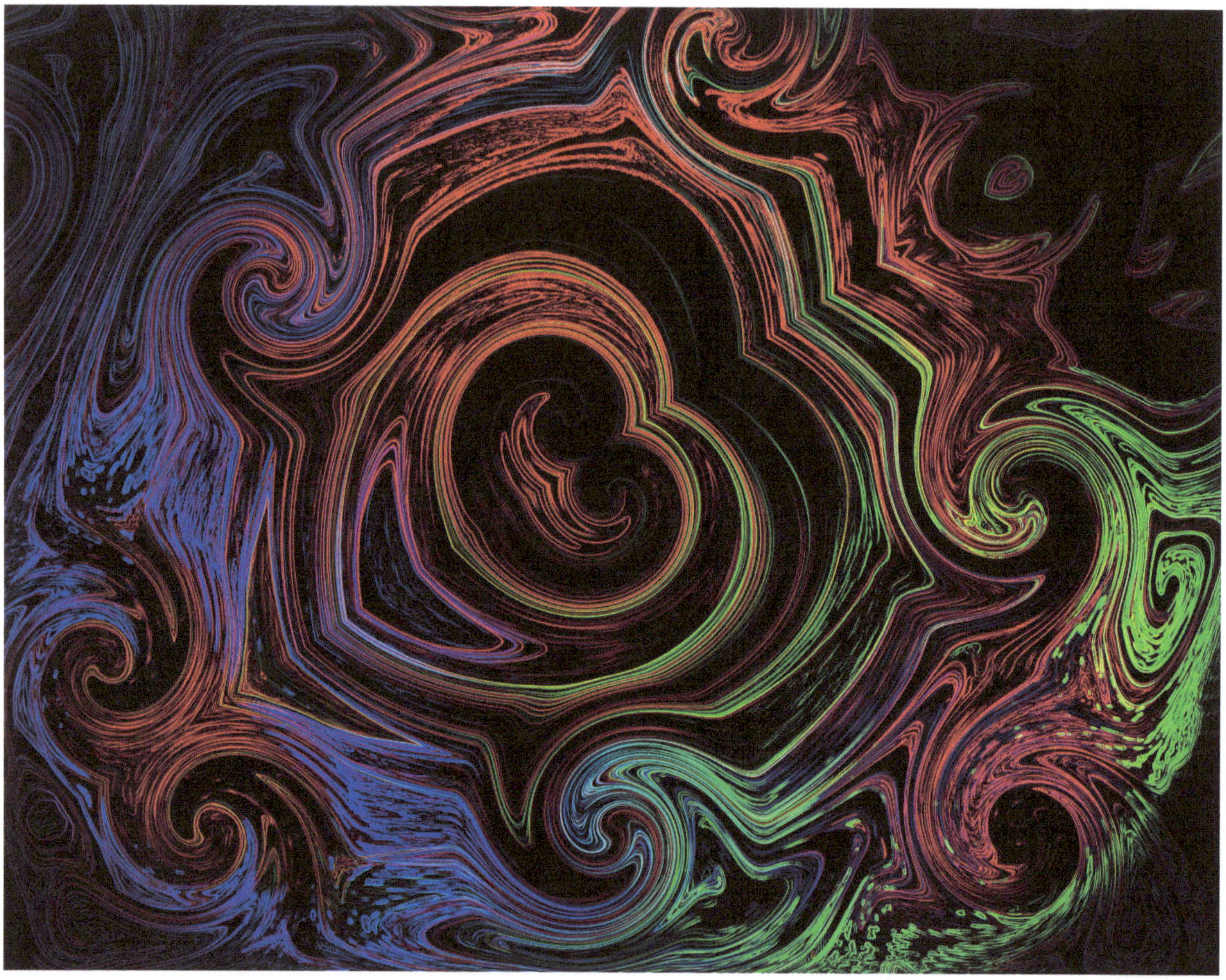

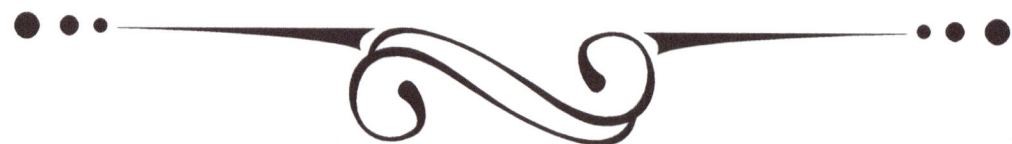

THE FORGE

The Forge is a fire burning away all impurities and hardens to steel. One flaw in the Forge and the instrument shatters like glass. Every heart must face the Forge.

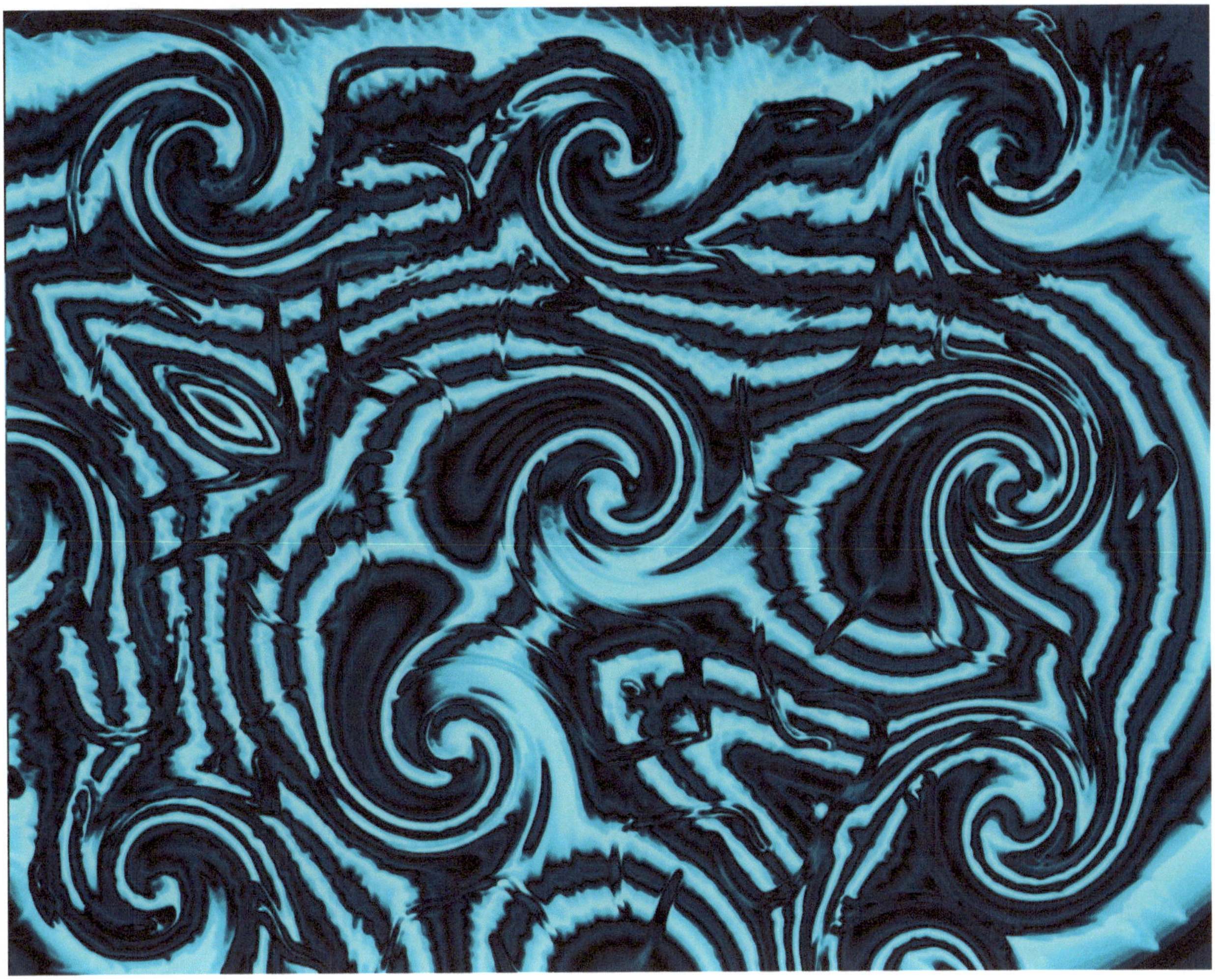

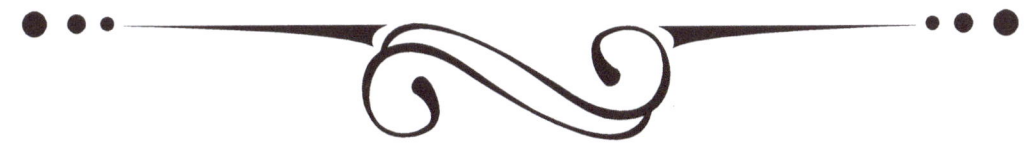

CRYSTAL SENTINEL

The Crystal sentinel sleeps as he guards the gates of reality and dreams the world yet to come.

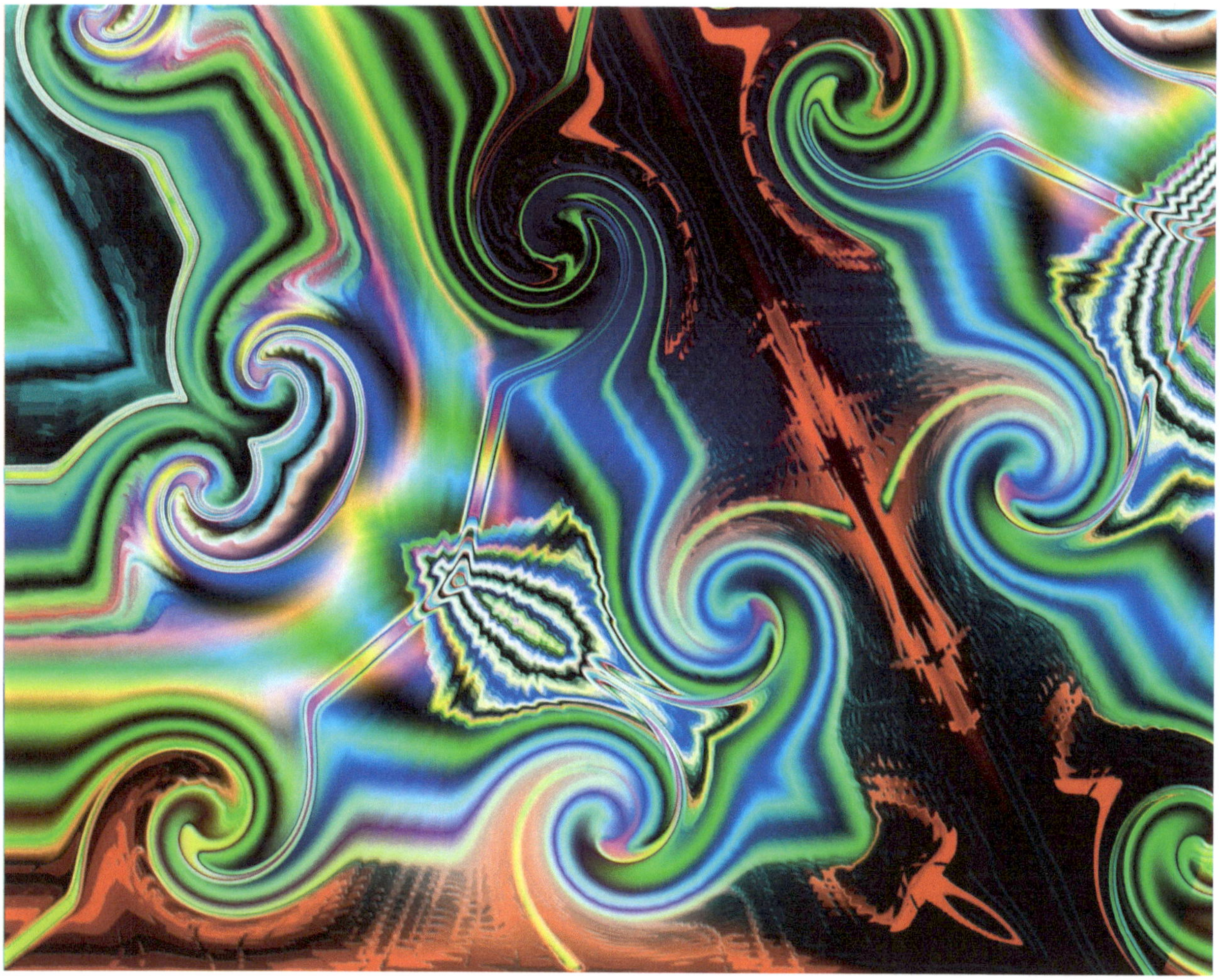

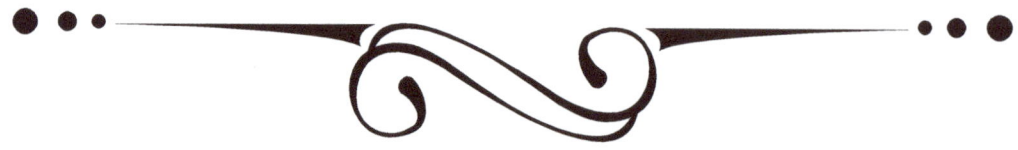

THE BEAST OF THE LUMINESCENT SEA

In the luminous sea, the most beautiful of places. There are always predators waiting to feed on the unsuspecting.

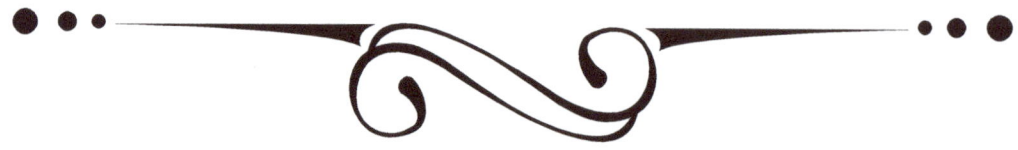

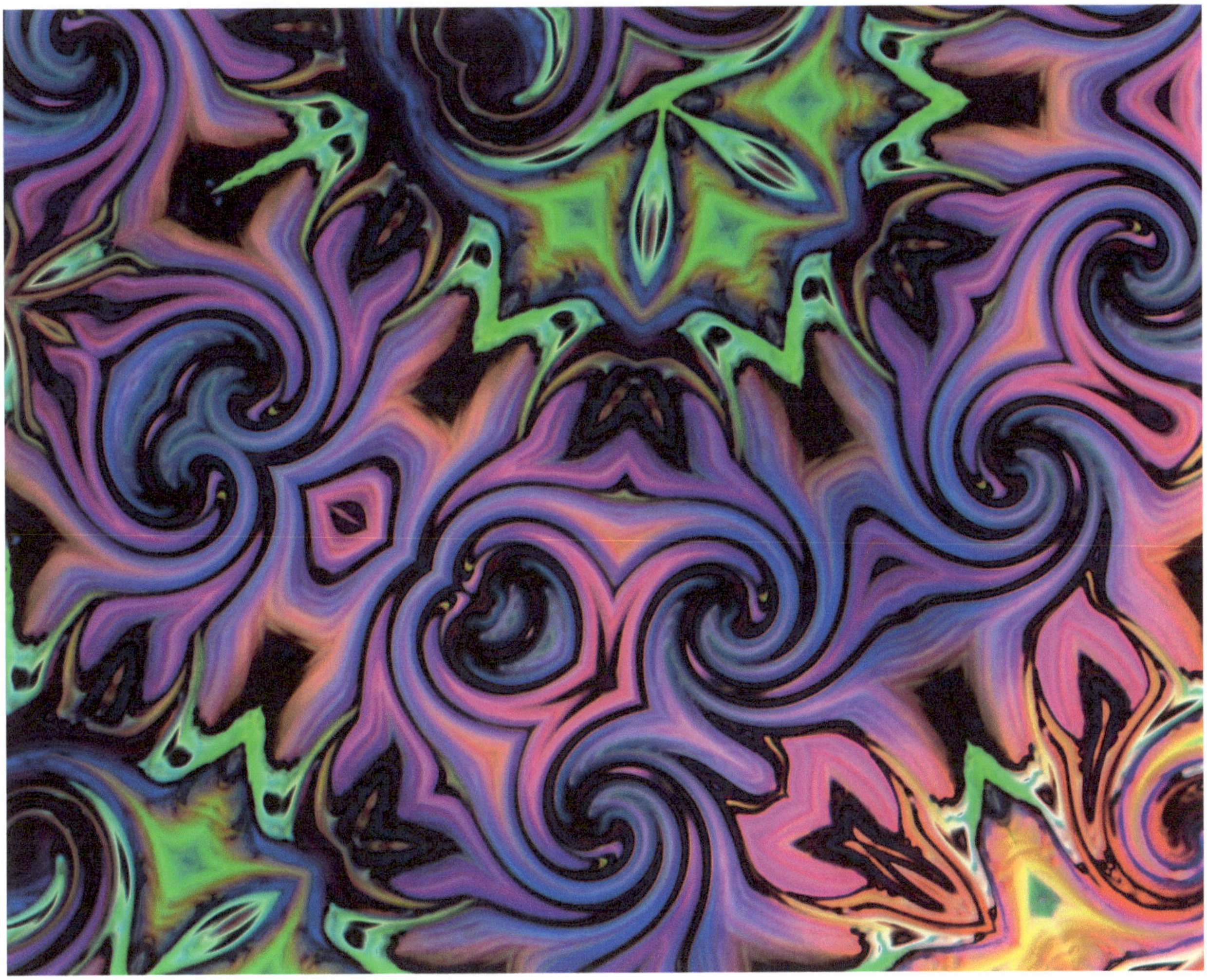

![Psychedelic swirling pattern artwork]

OASIS OF THE DIVERGENT

A place of beauty and rest then you take a closer look. Are those eyes? Did that move? Or is it just mental divergence.

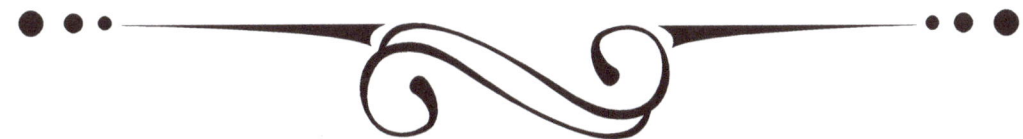

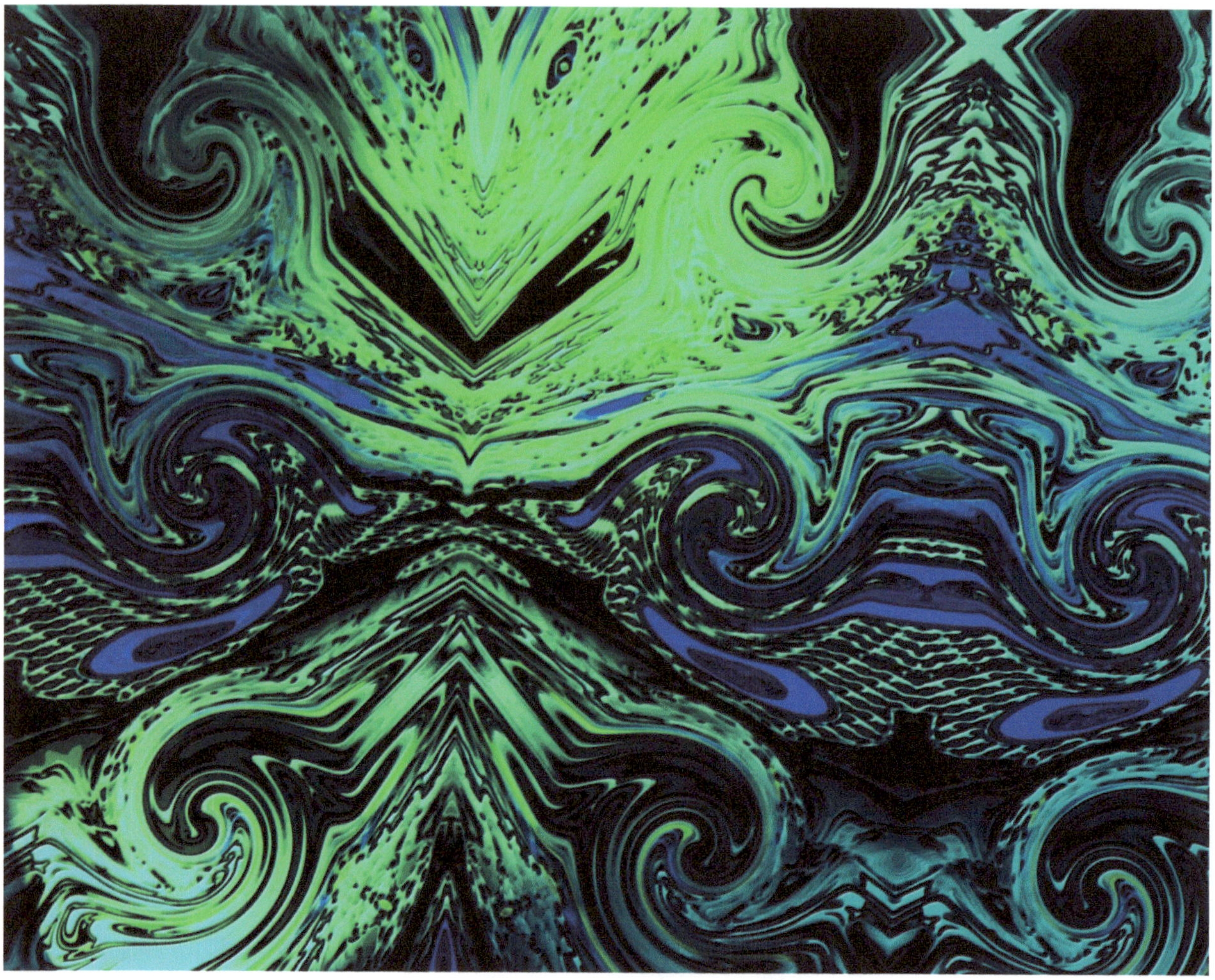

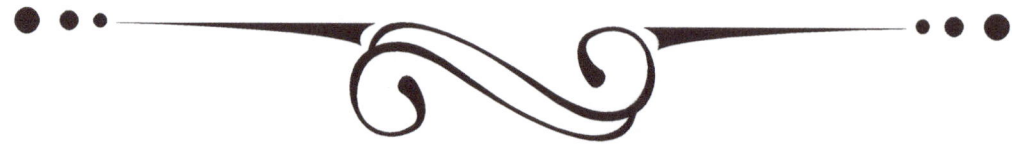

TIMES FORGOTTEN GUARDIANS

All too often it seems as we break ground to build the modern we uncover times lost guardians in the foundation.

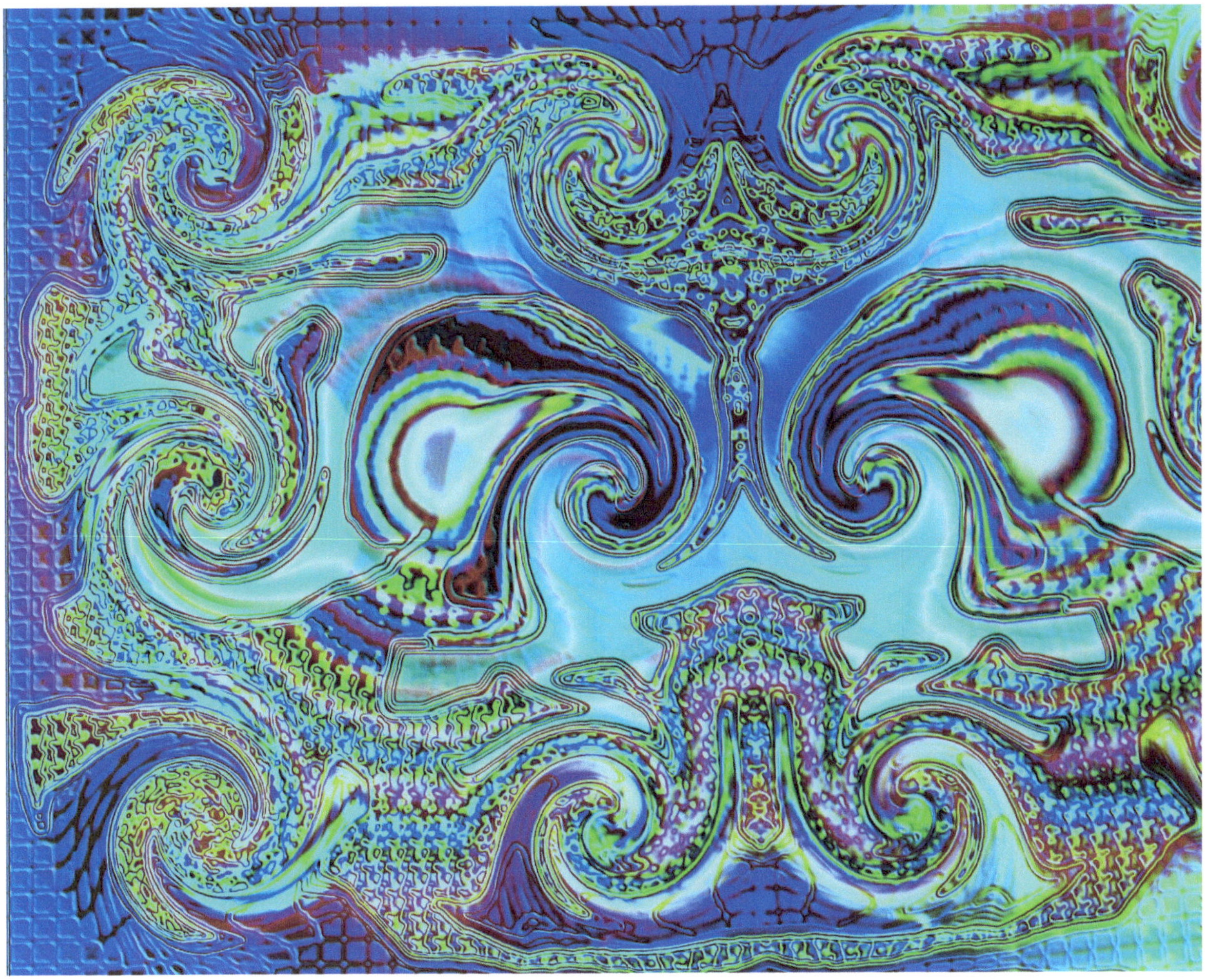

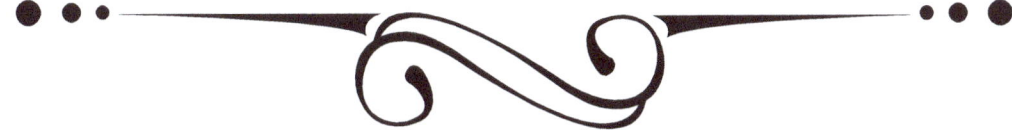

BOREAS

I am the Northern wind, the frost maker, and the thunderhead all freeze beneath my gaze. I am a Boreas.

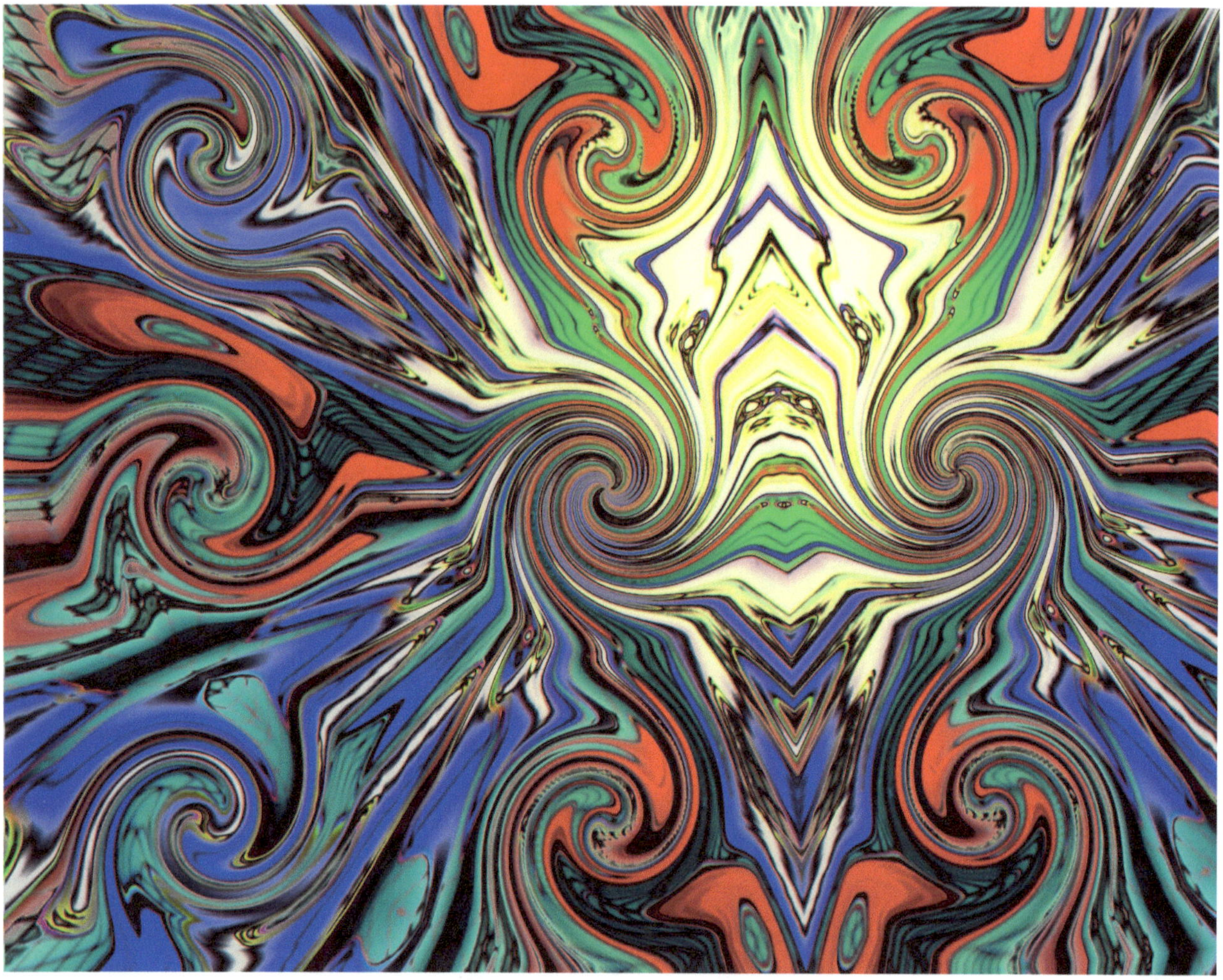

SONG OF CREATION

First, there was the sound; The sound turned to light, color, and line, The form of creation.

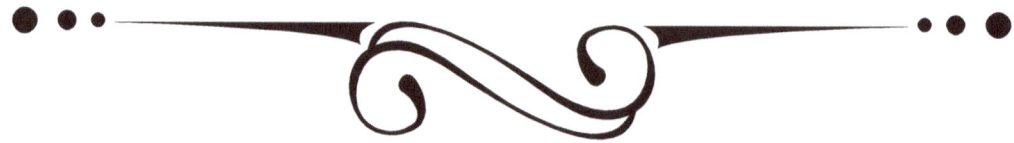

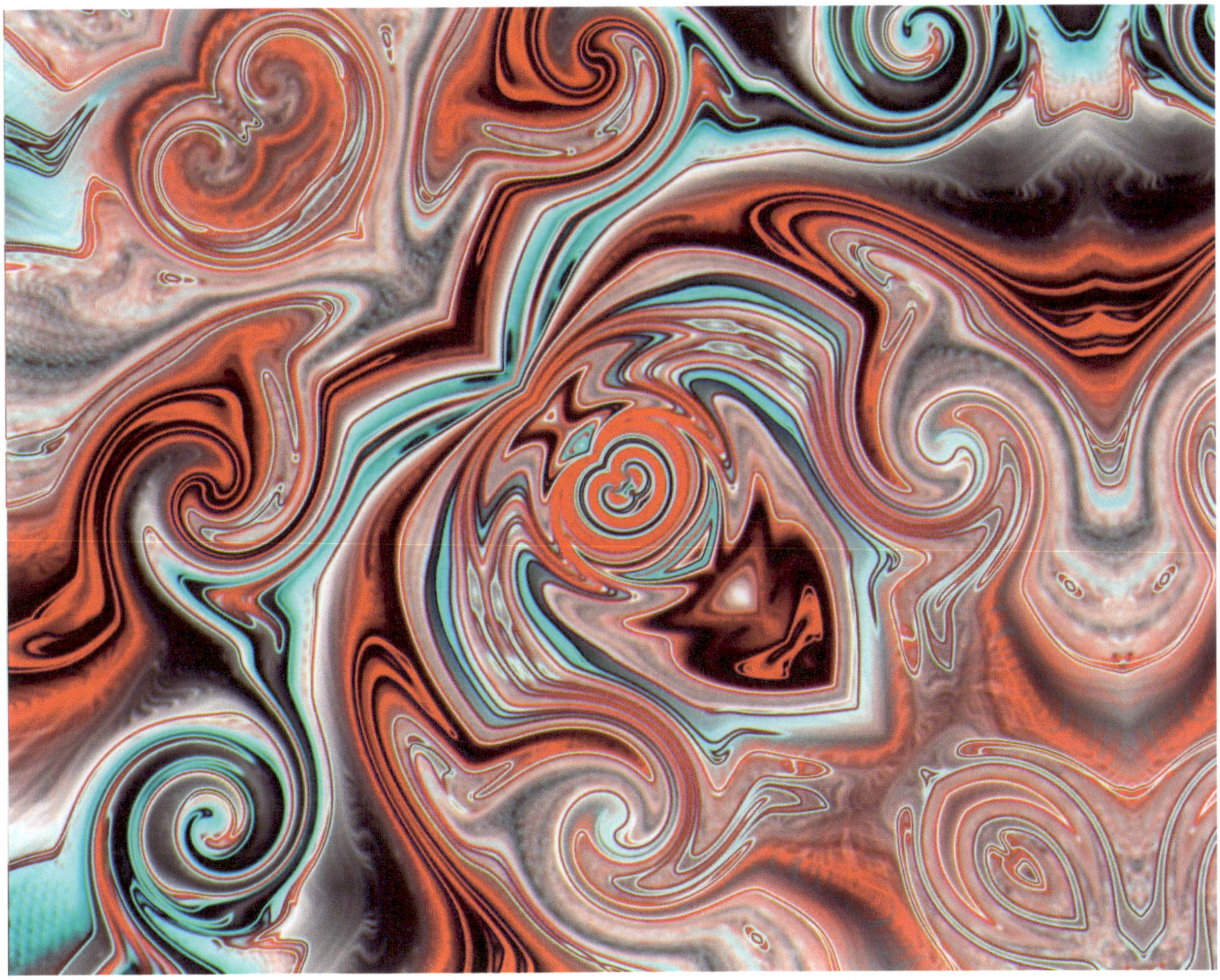

![Abstract swirled marbled pattern in orange, teal, black, and white]

CUMBERSOME THRONE

The cumbersome throne of self-rule carries weight and reveals nobility shown with the deeply carved lines of time.

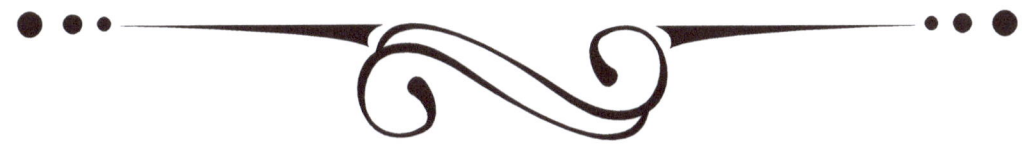

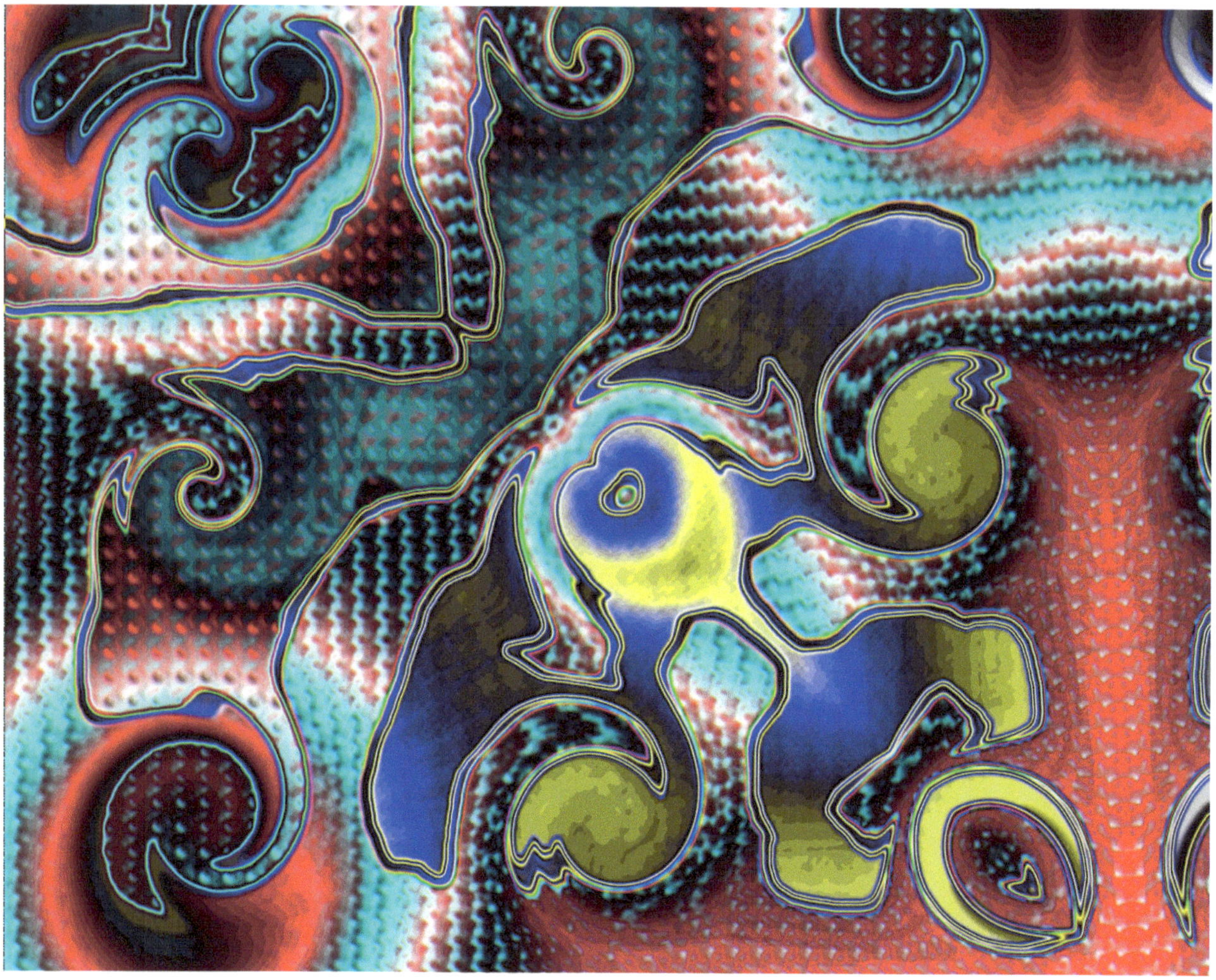

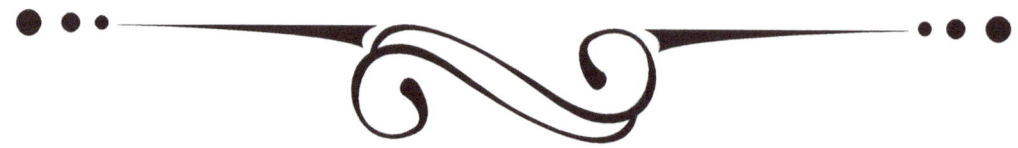

RESENTMENT OF THE OPPUGNED

Primal cold rage of retaliation is inborn amongst ancient foes. Locked forever is the resentment of the oppugned.

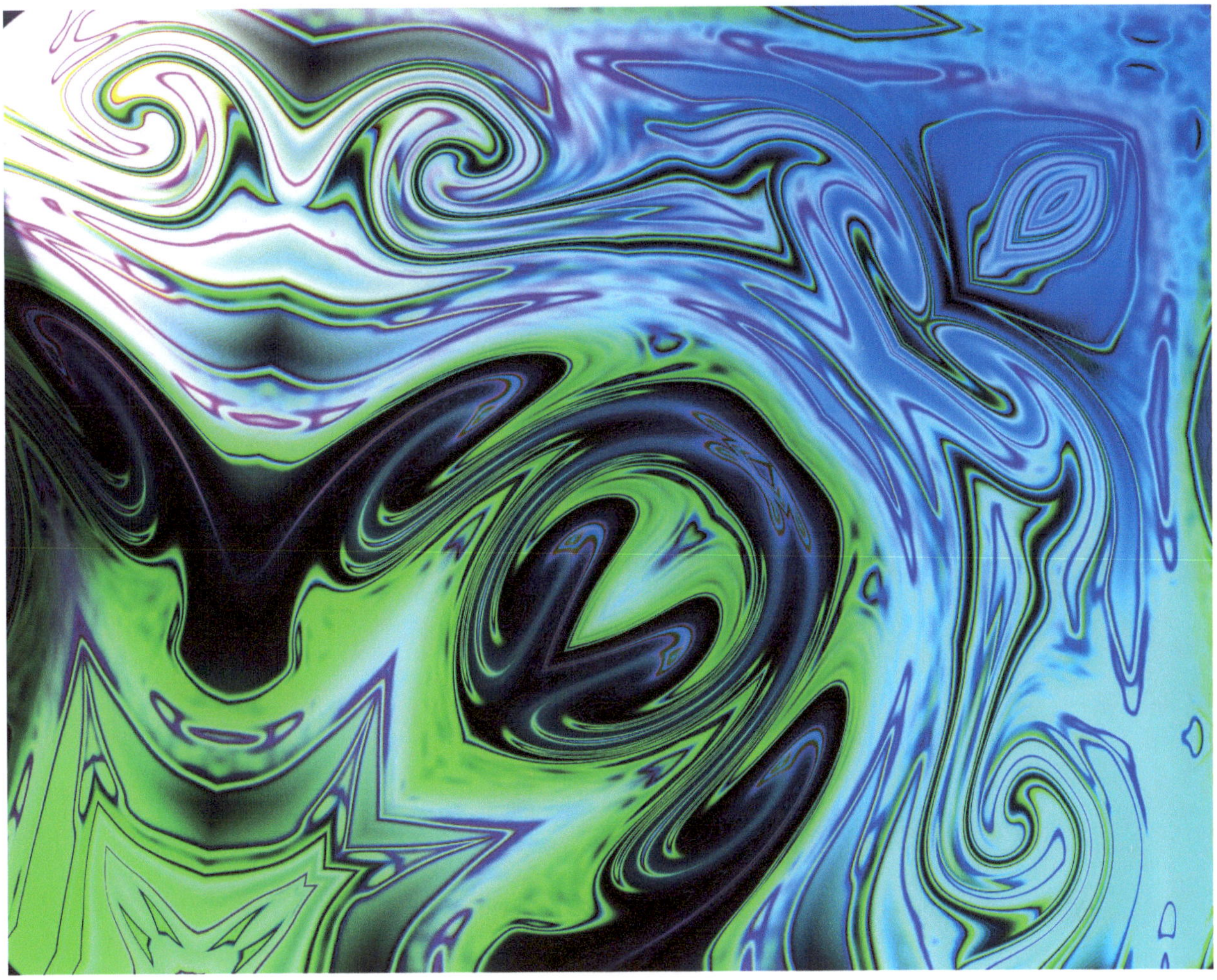

EIDOLA

That glimpse out of the corner of your eye, The feeling you are never alone. Look long and hard enough, and you will see the Eidola are with you.

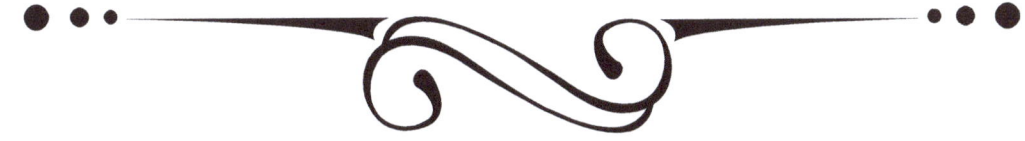

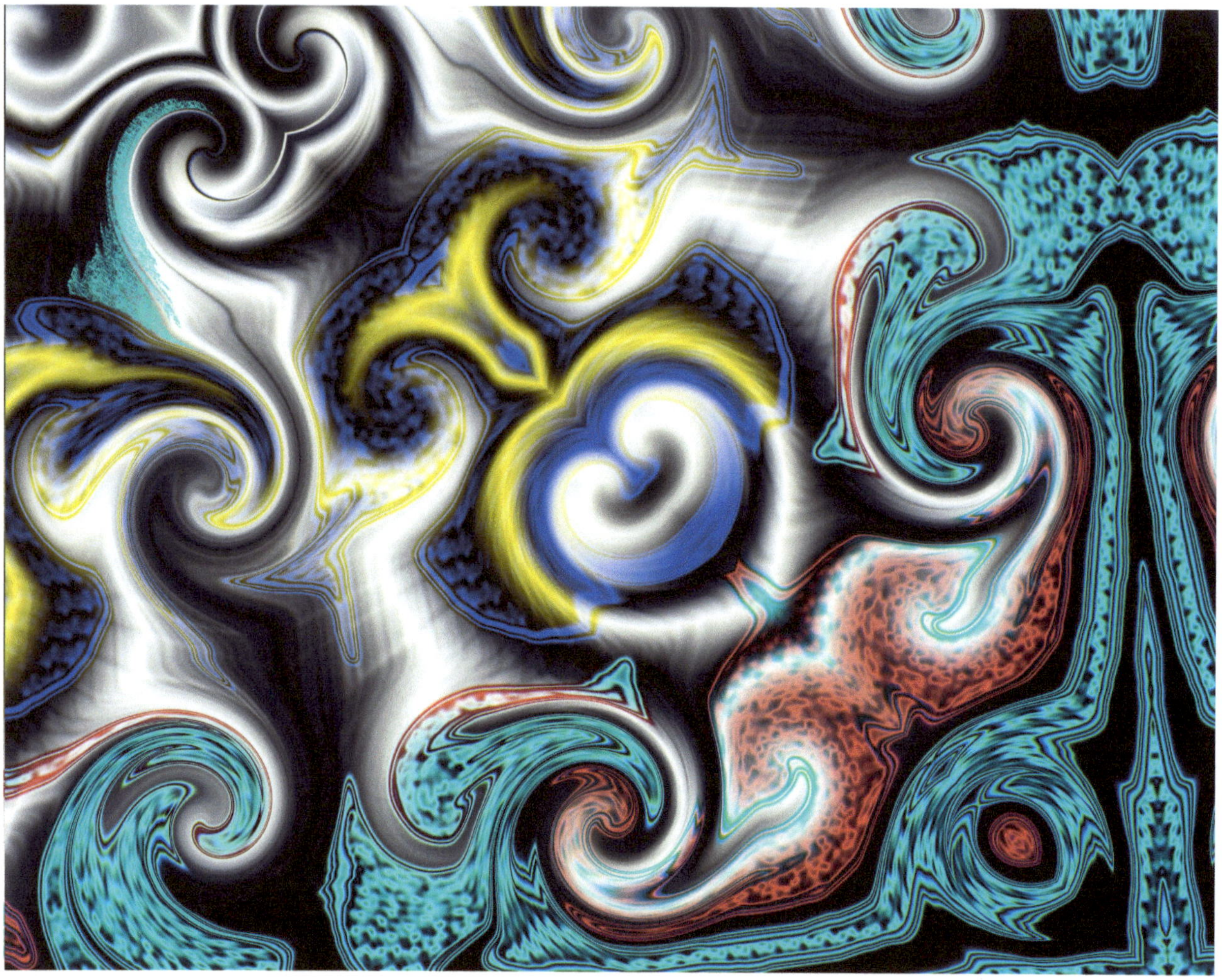

![Abstract swirling artwork with spirals in white, blue, yellow, teal, and orange tones]

PHALANX PRIME

In close formation protecting what is right and noble in the human heart, This is Phalanx Prime.

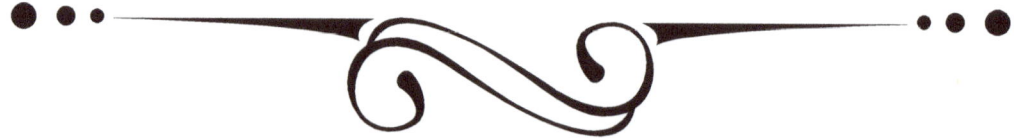

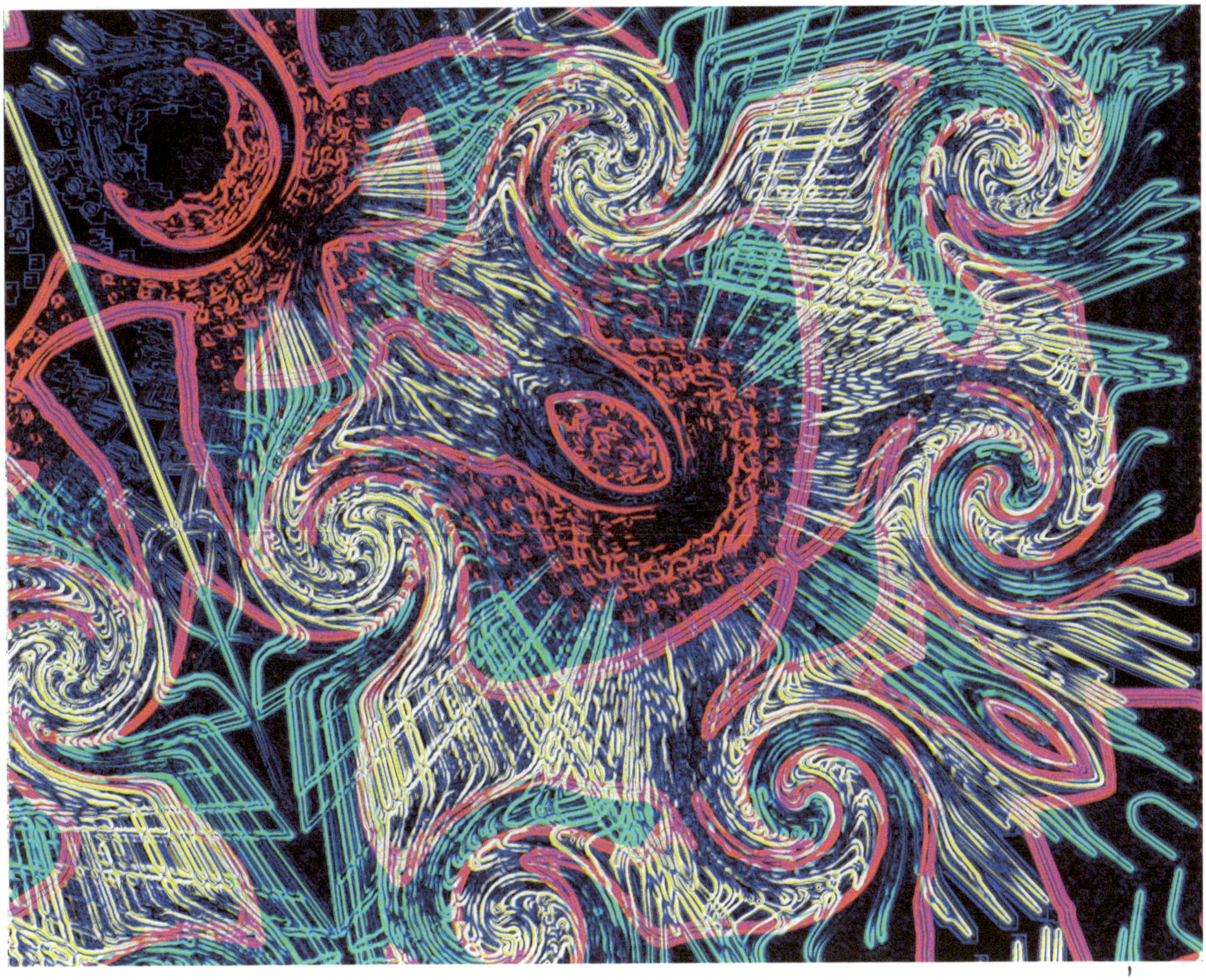

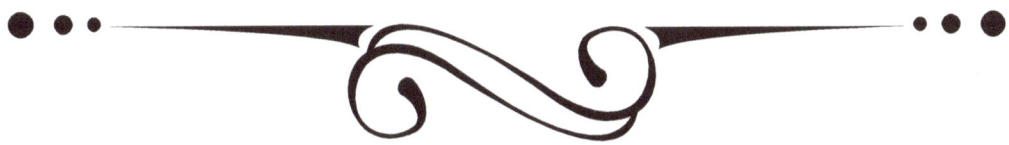

EXALTED TRIUMPHANT

When forceful lines gather, and you find yourself moving with a power beyond your own, you will gaze upon the Exalted triumphant.

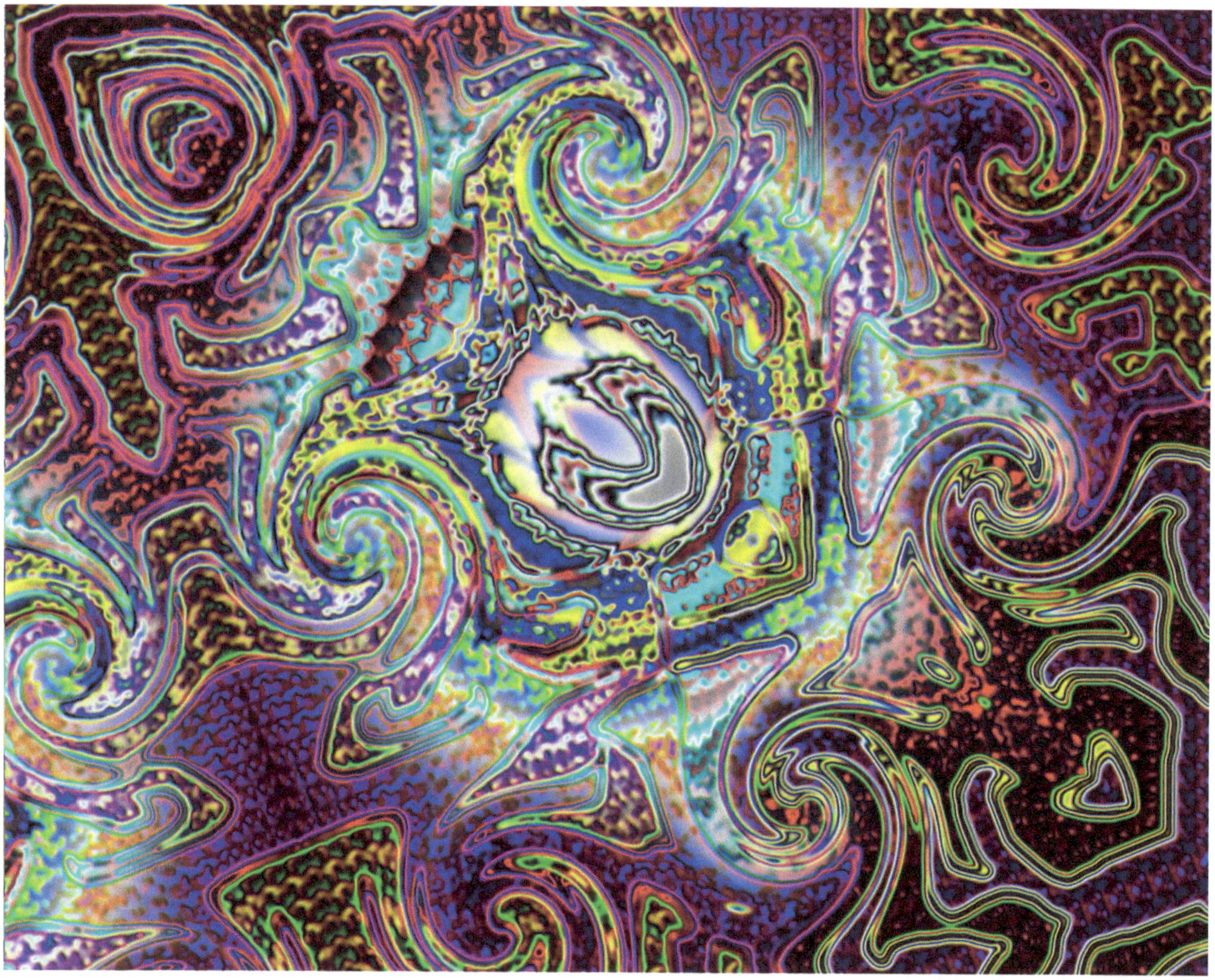

AND CHAOS LAUGHED

The very fact may be what we call order is chaos and chaos may be the correct universal order.

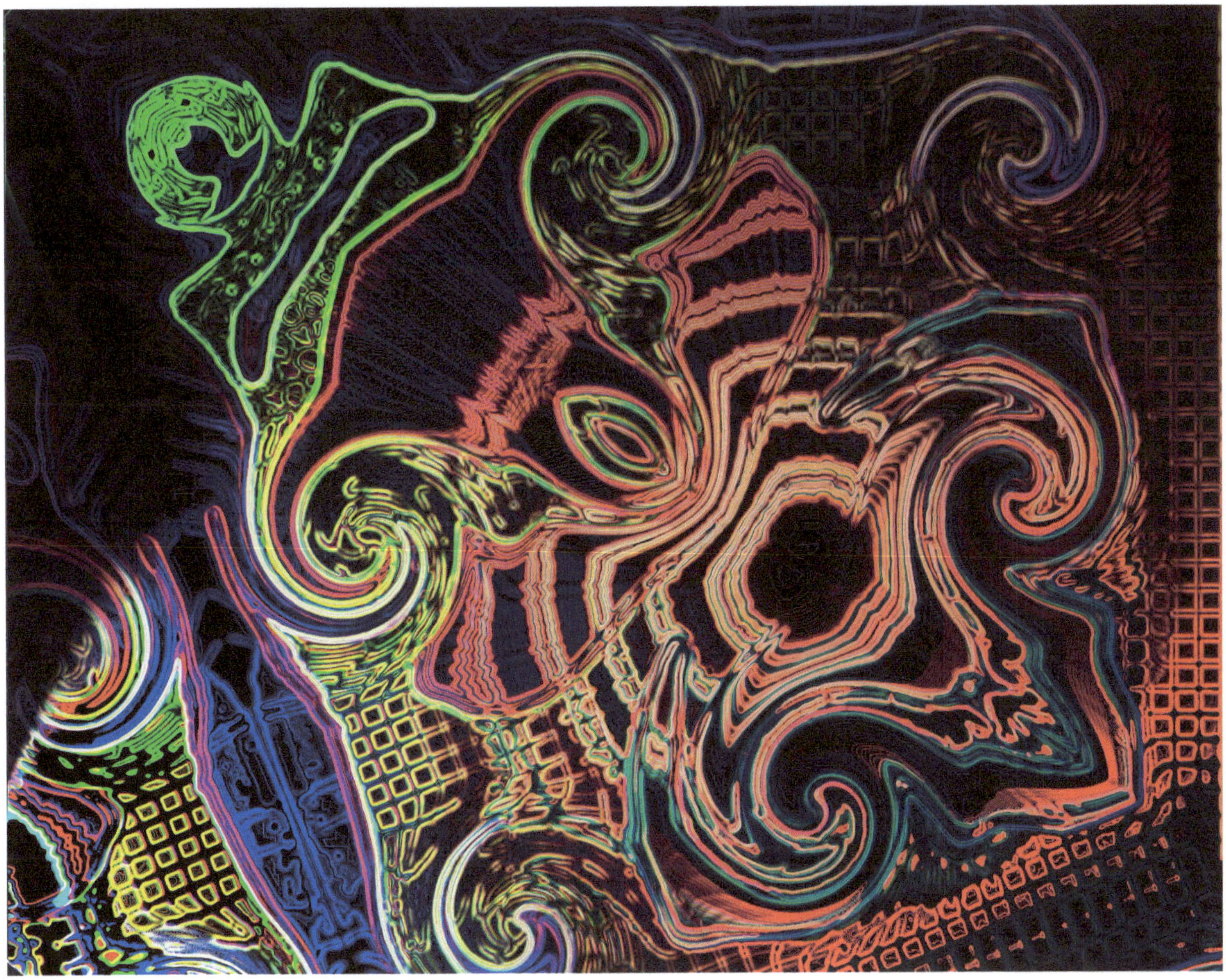

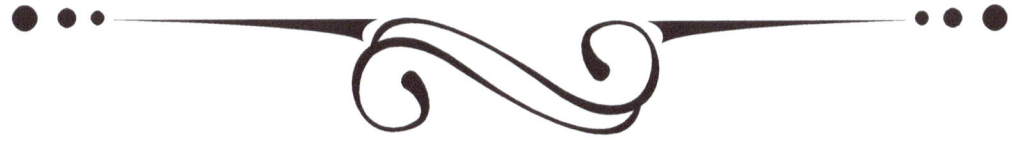

THE 4TH SEAL

When he had opened the fourth seal, I heard the voice of the fourth beast say, Come and see. As I gazed down into the pool, I saw the creature was me.

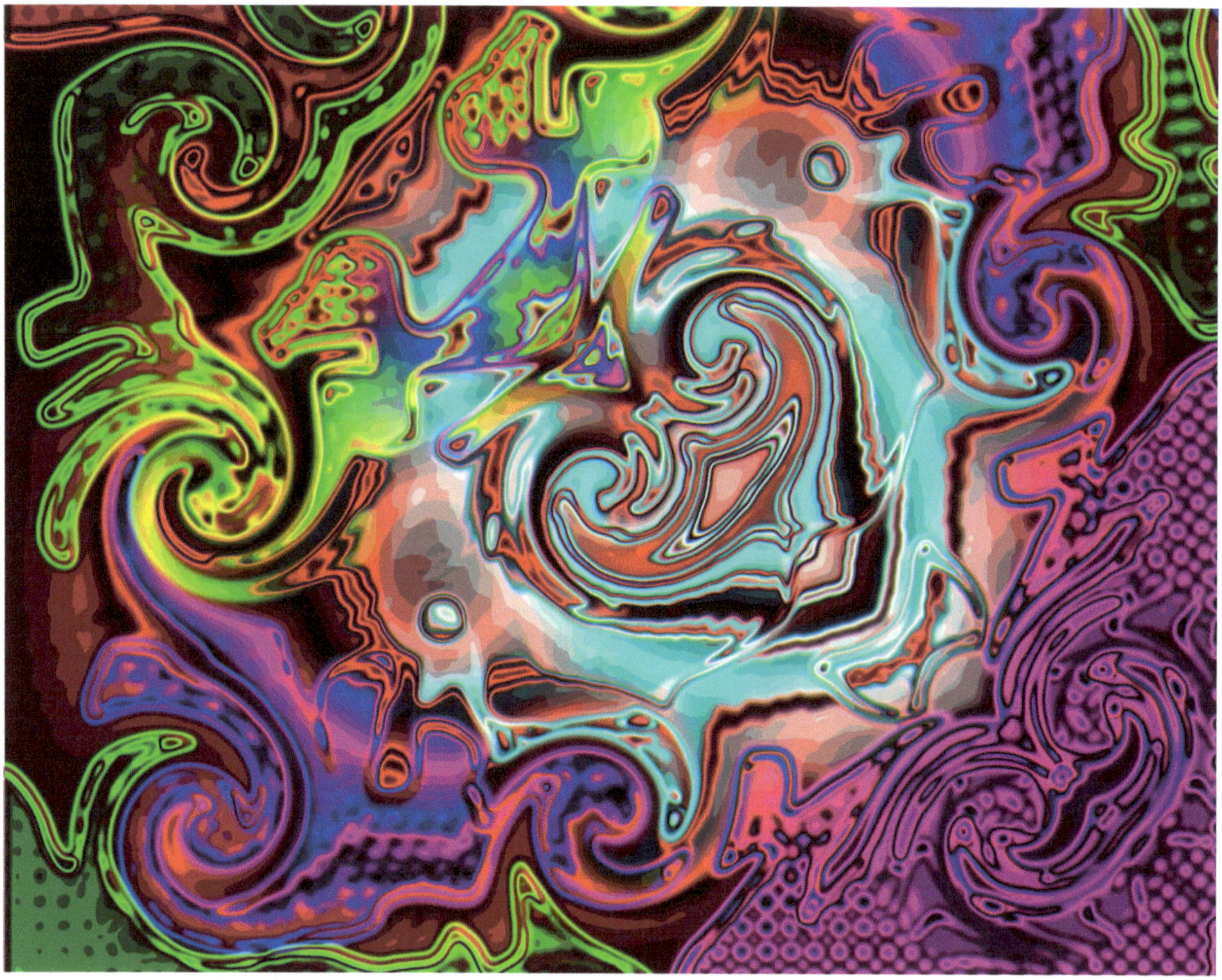

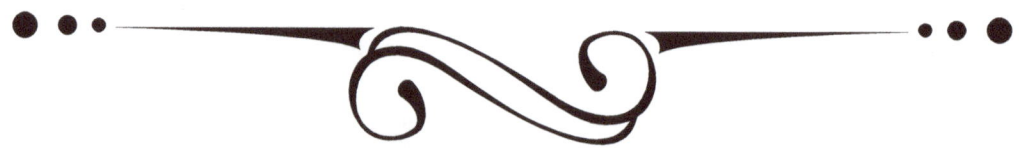

REPENTANCE

This work went through many evolutions before reaching its final form. Ever-changing light color and form much like the path to repentance many things must change to reach the last point.

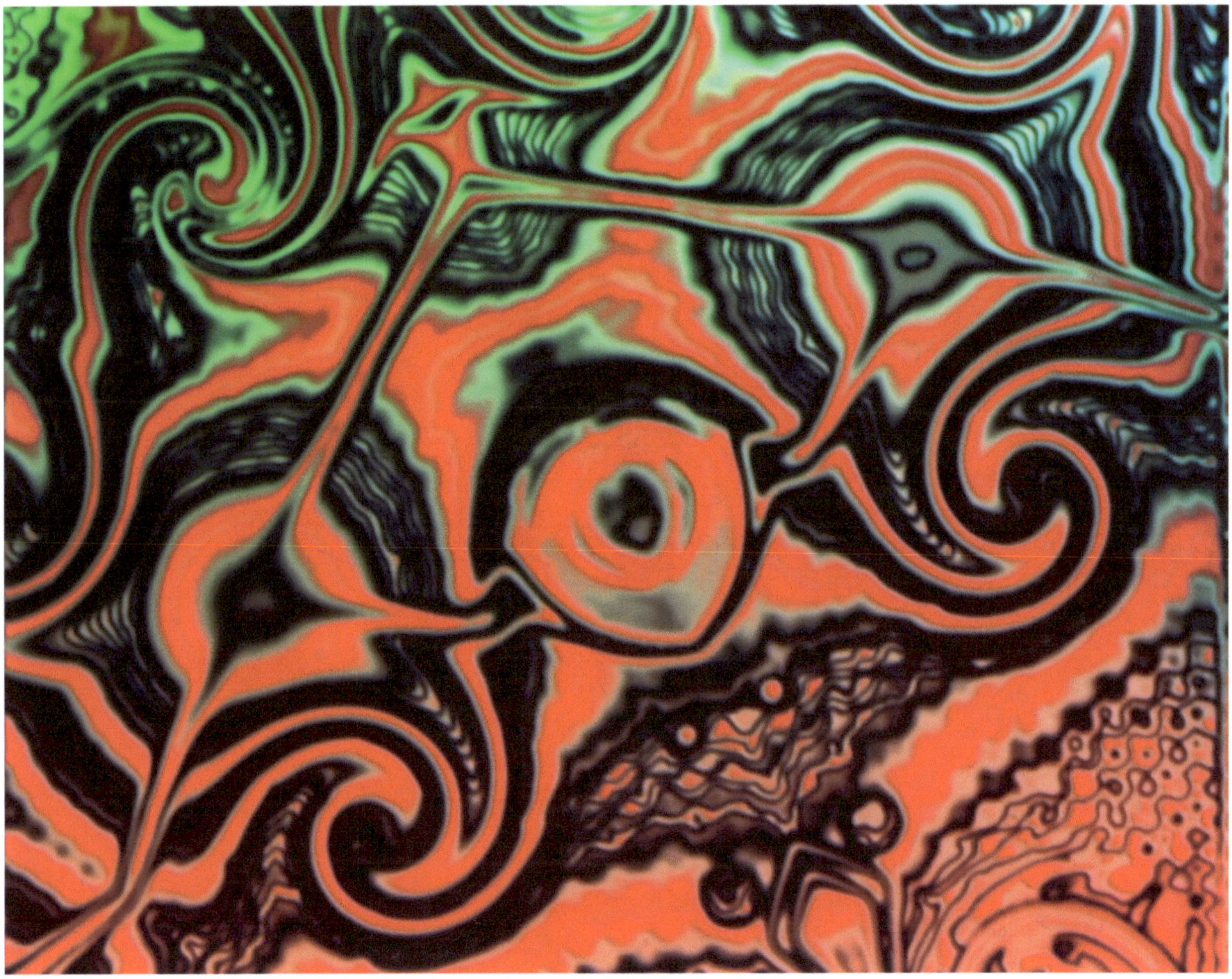

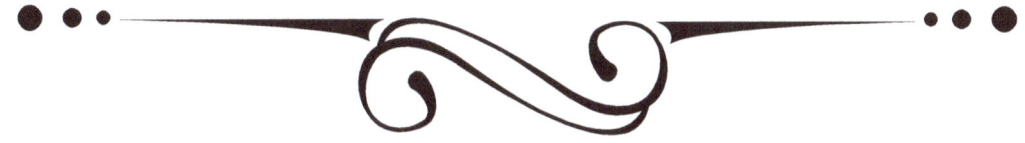

IN DEEP TIME

I have looked in deep time and seen that which is old and compelling. I serve as a bridge for the most ancient of things to assert its will into the modern digital.

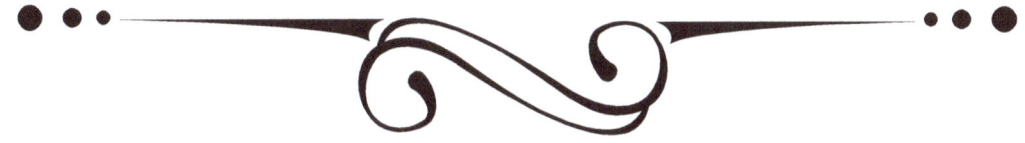

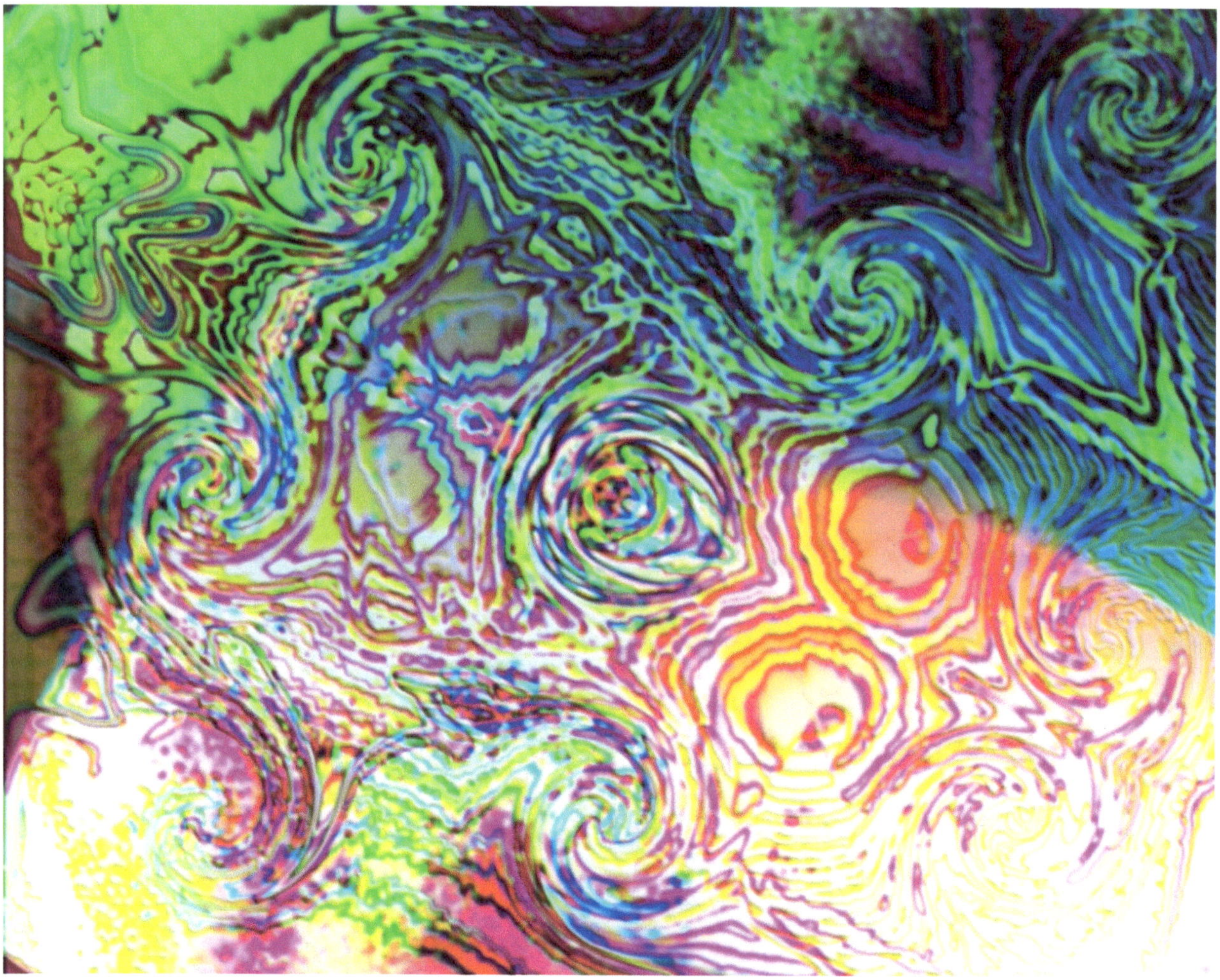

![A swirling, vibrantly colored abstract image with green, blue, purple, yellow, and red tones]

A CRY FROM BEYOND

Looking beyond the veil of what we see and hear every day there are times you catch a glimpse of a place of light and sounds that are unknown to you, and you hear a cry from beyond, The absolute strangeness of that experience compelled me to create and share the image.

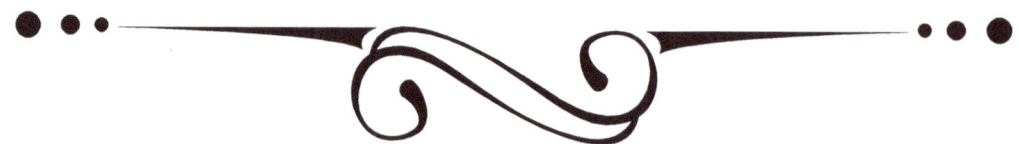

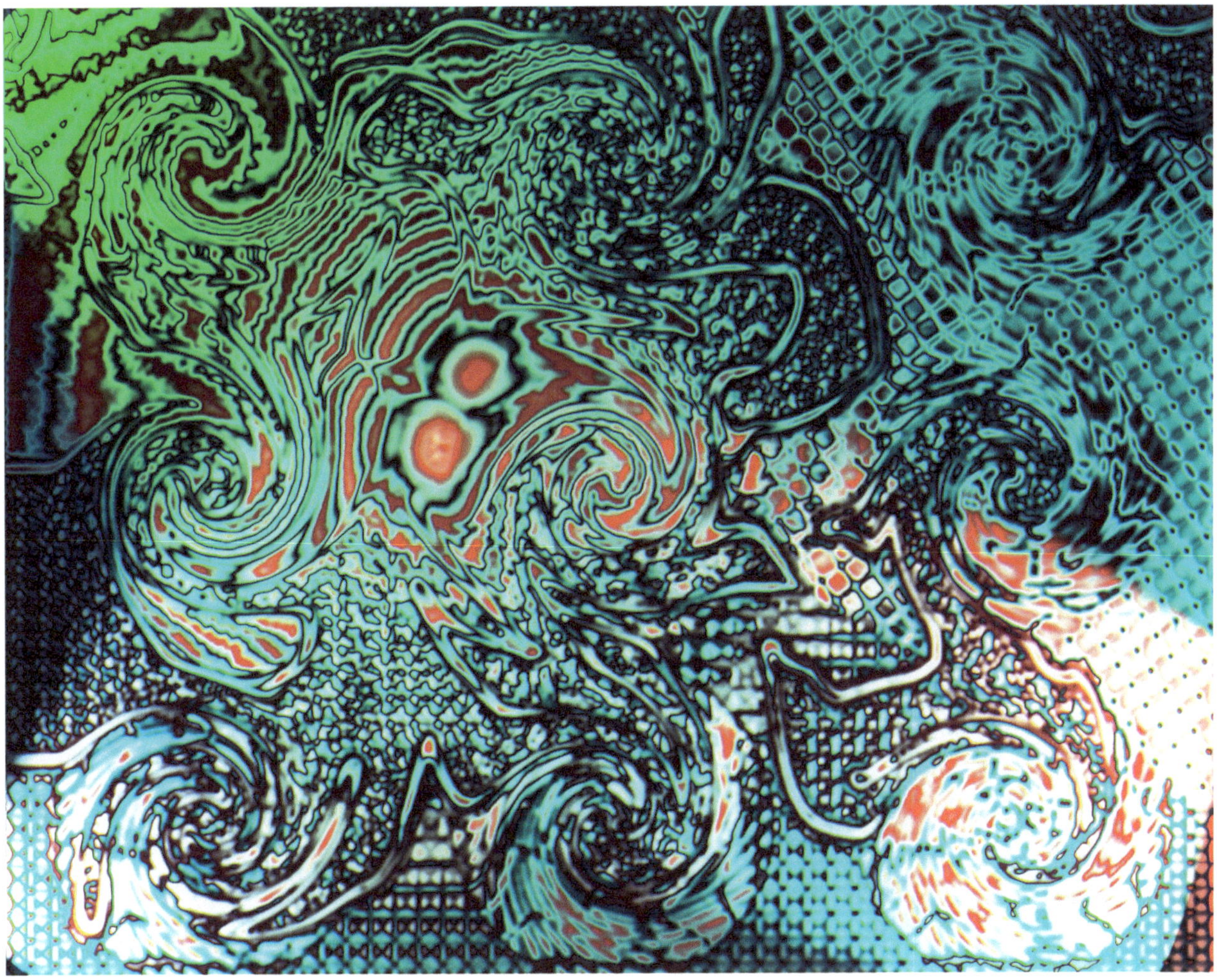

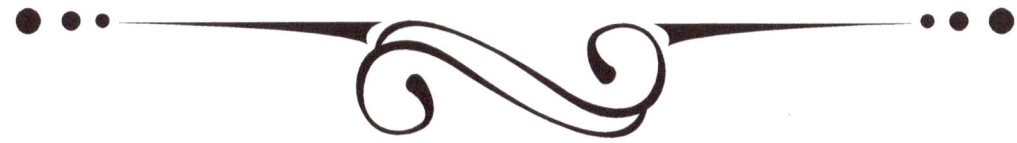

NEAR LANDS END

I let my mind drift away from humanity and looked out over the endless sea of my consciousness. I said to myself. I see lands end, and there be monsters.

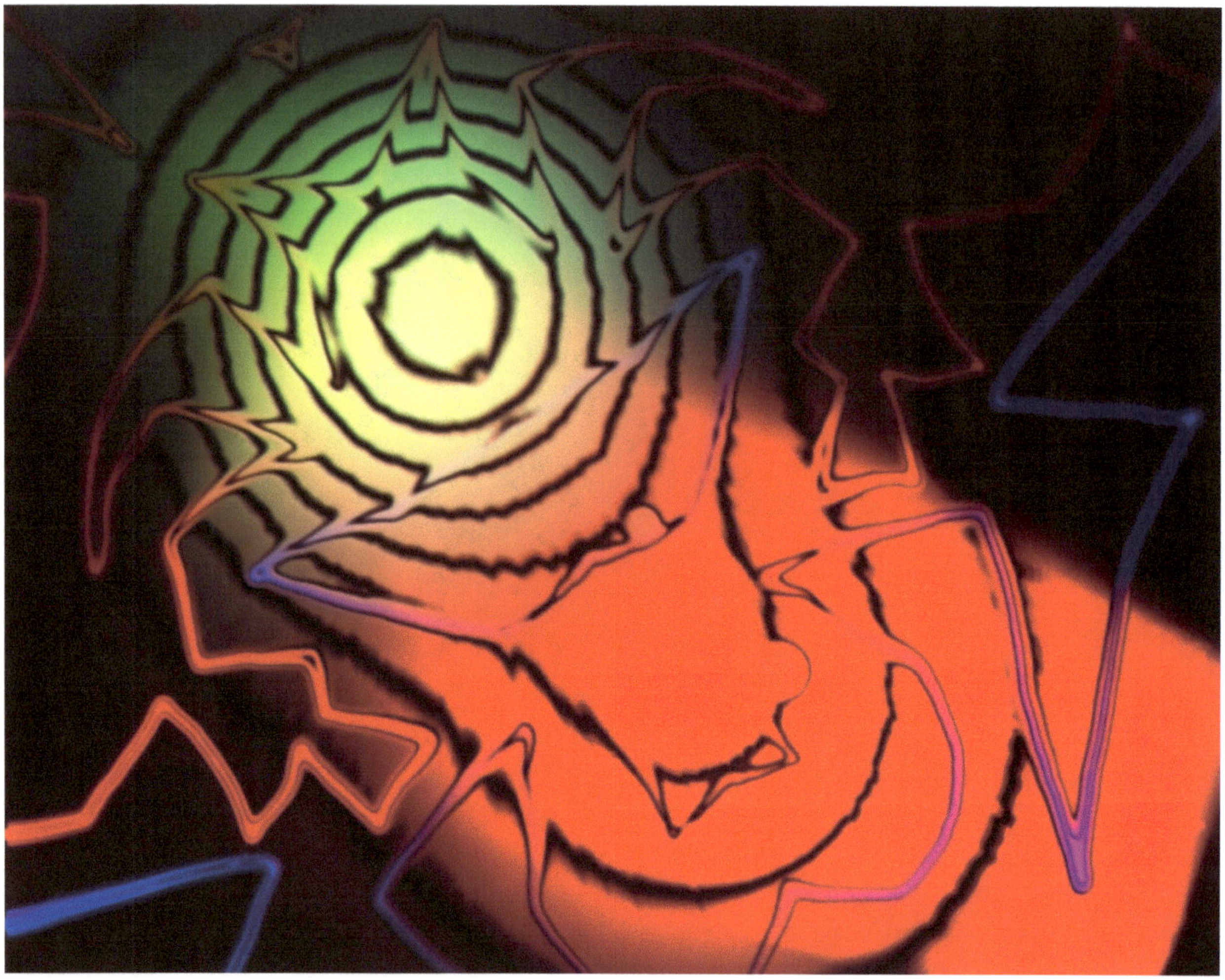

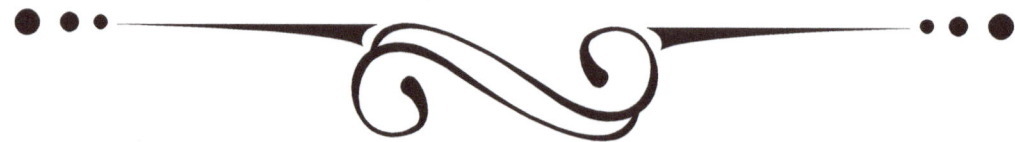

THE ABYSS LOOKS BACK AT YOU

Reminded of my mortality and all the near misses with death, I have lived through my living work of art directed its growth to give me the apparent answer to what happens when you look into the abyss.

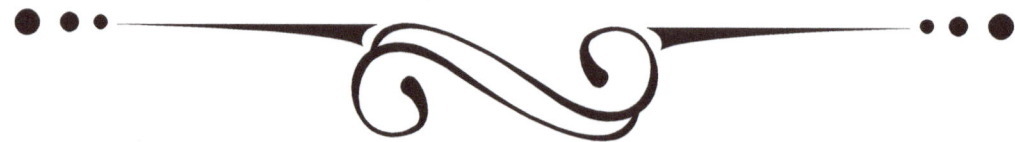

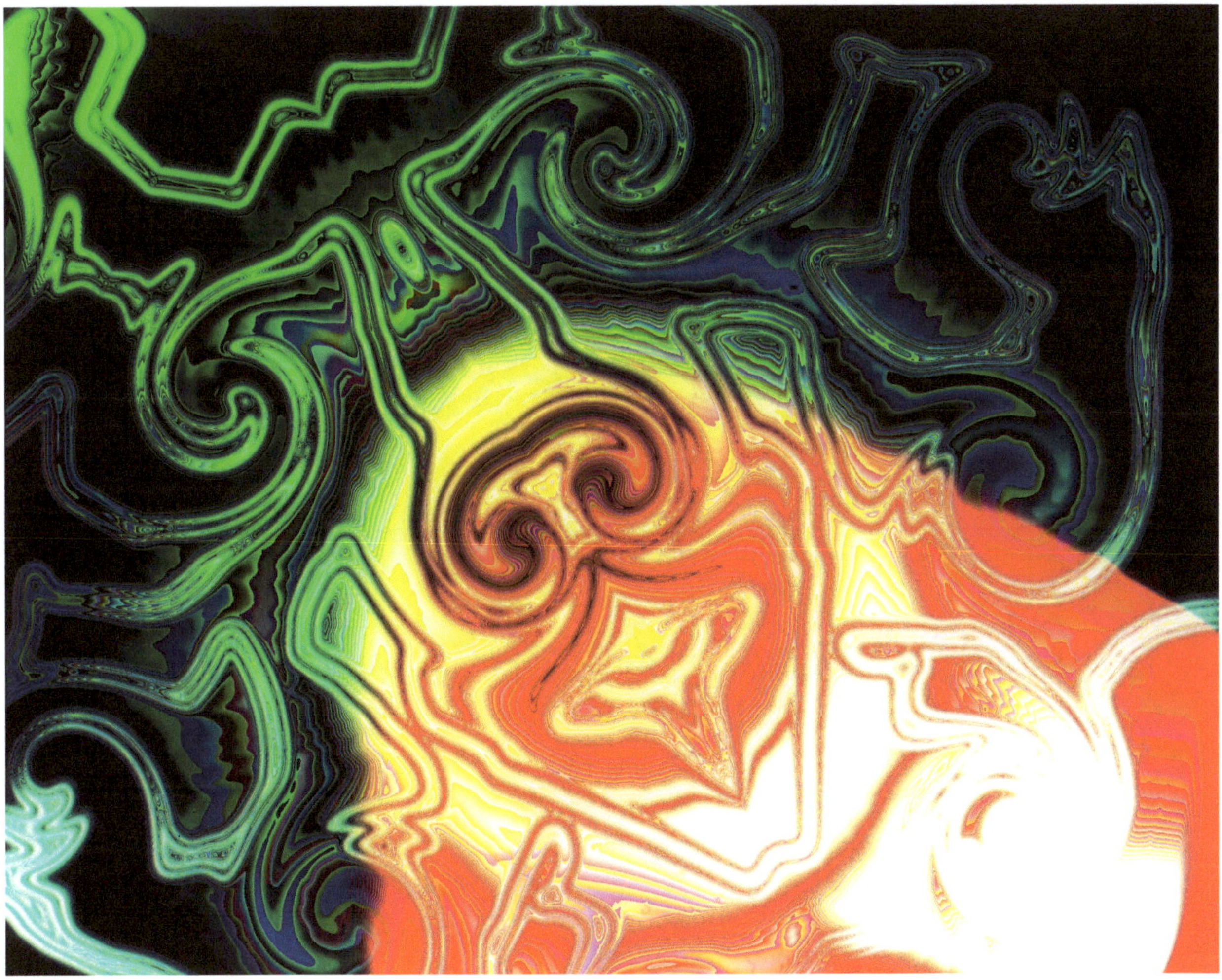

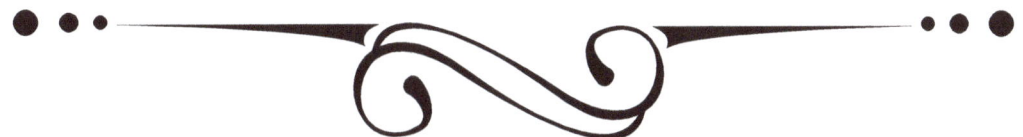

SOVEREIGN

Sovereign is the force of mind the drives all humans to make sense out of the universe. Monarch is the subconscious that drives the hand of the creator.

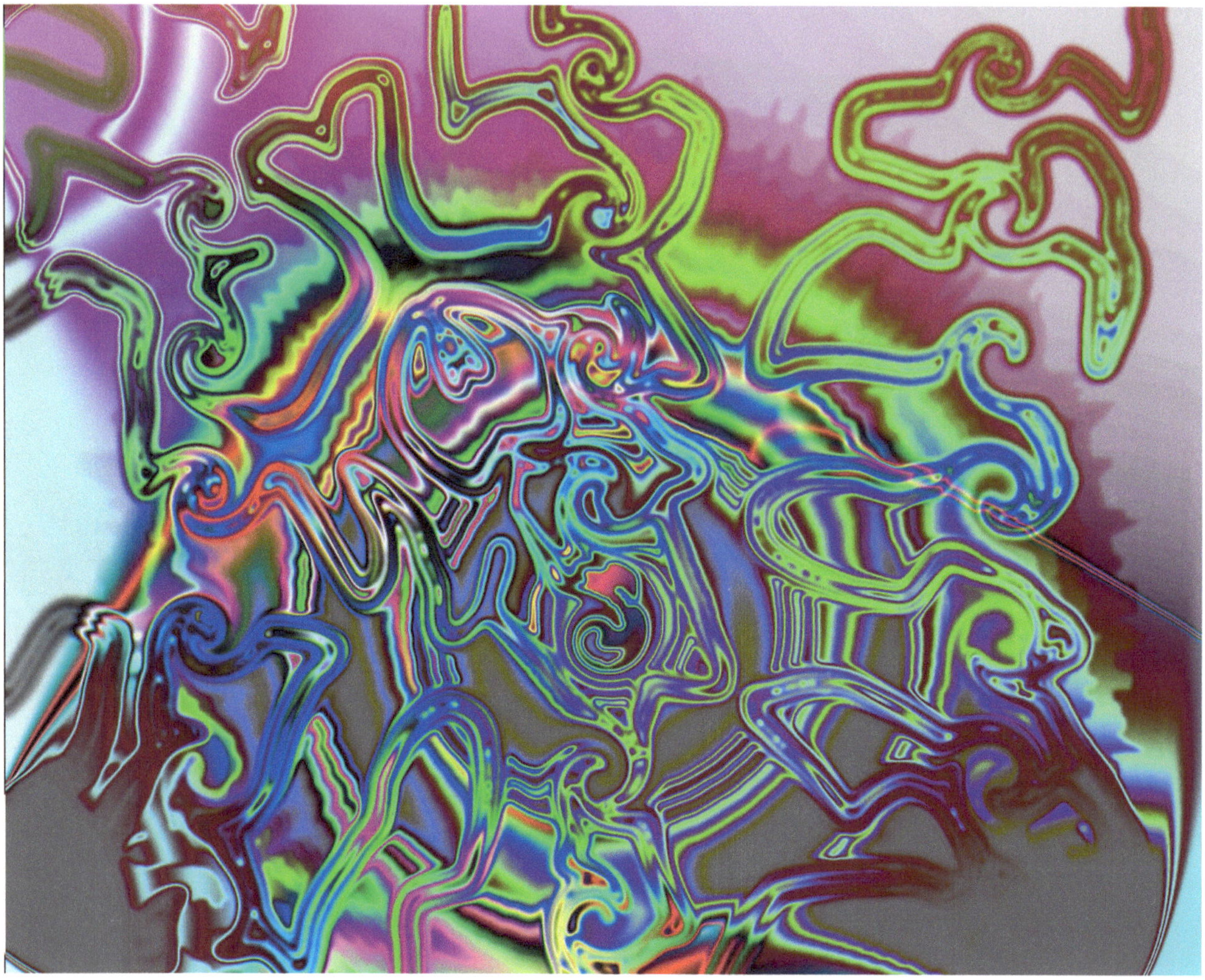

DOLOMEDES

Dolomedes evolved much like its watery home fluid and taking on a life of its own. I knew my work is done when I could feel the life flow from the work.

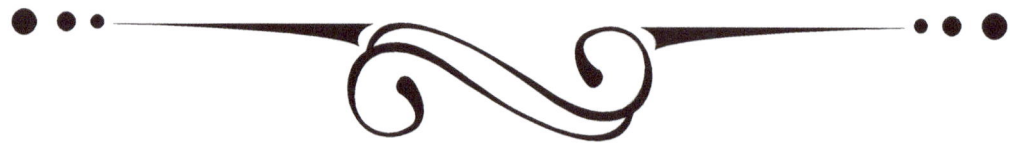

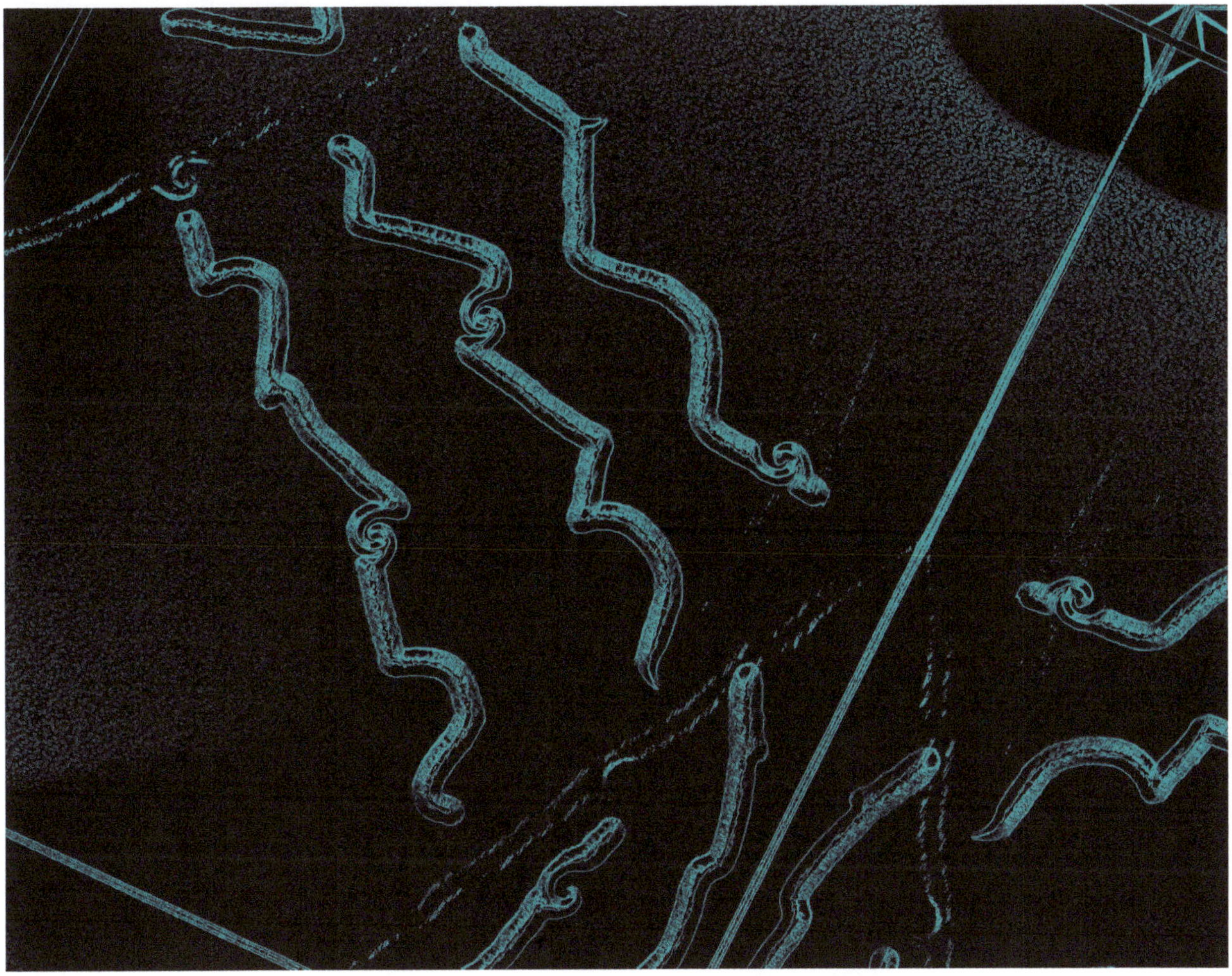

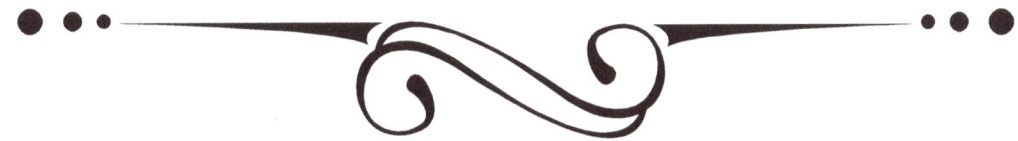

DISILLUSION

I was reminded of my time in the U.S Army. I went to many places no one should go and saw many things no one should see. It was the first time I had felt disillusion I realized I am not Immortal, and I am going to have to claw my way out of this to survive.

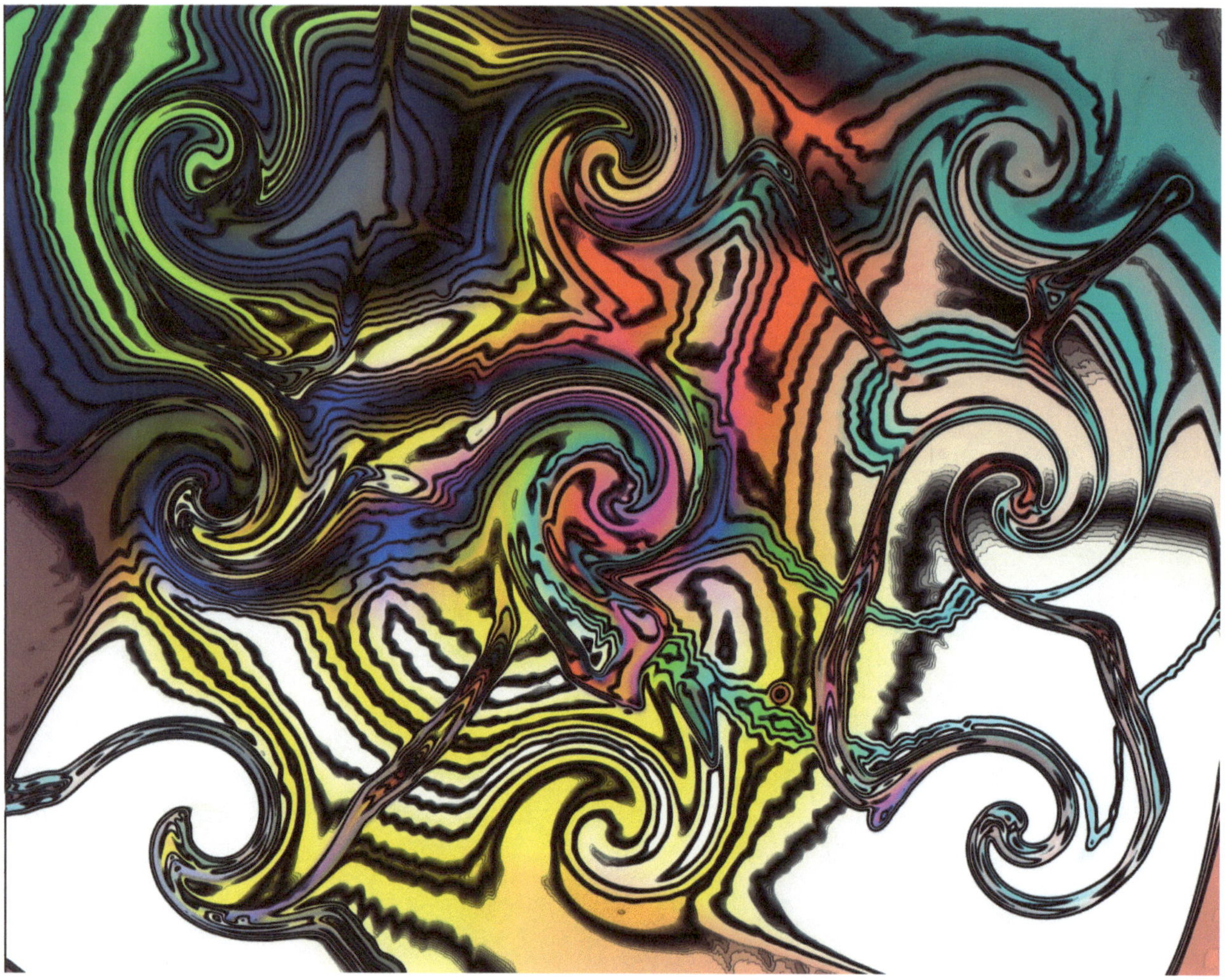

![Psychedelic abstract swirling image of Cthulhu]

CTHULHU

I saw the sky had shattered as Cthulhu descended from the split in the heavens. I felt the gaze of the old one and burned its presence into this Icon.

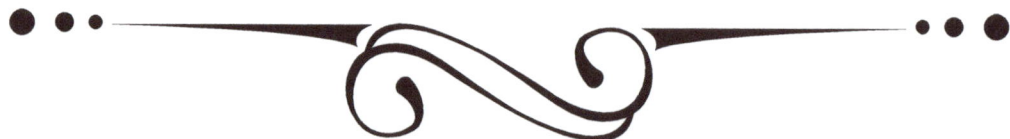

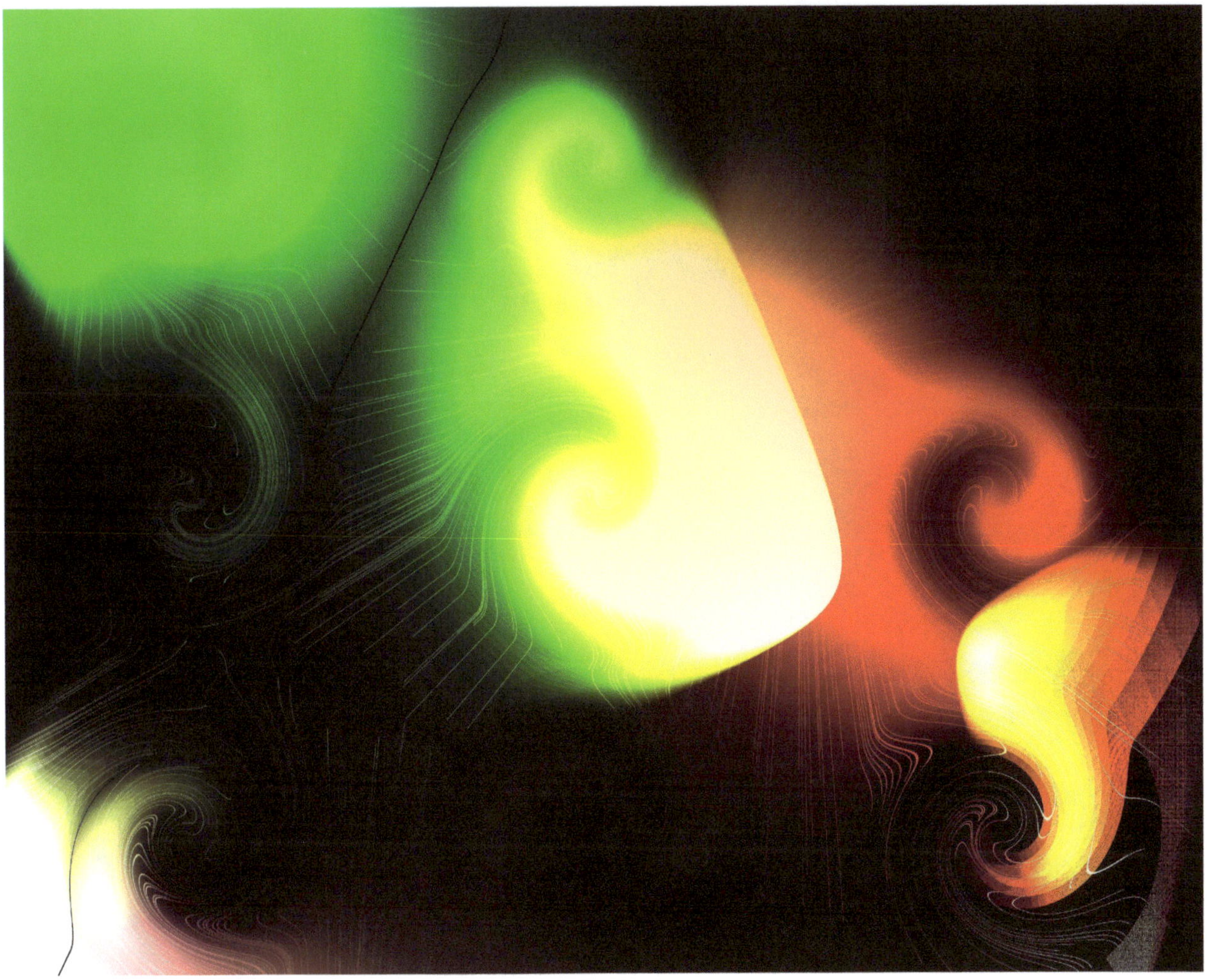

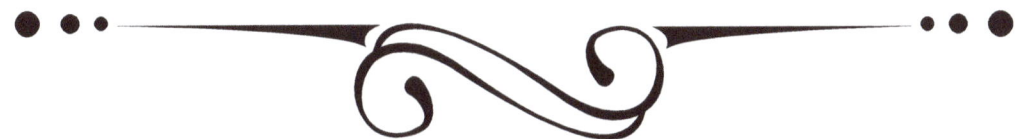

CONVERGENCE

When you work with abstracts in the digital medium, the piece seems to evolve and grow right before your eyes. When you get past the place of concentrating on technical skills and the forethought of 20 sketches to make one painting, you find Convergence.

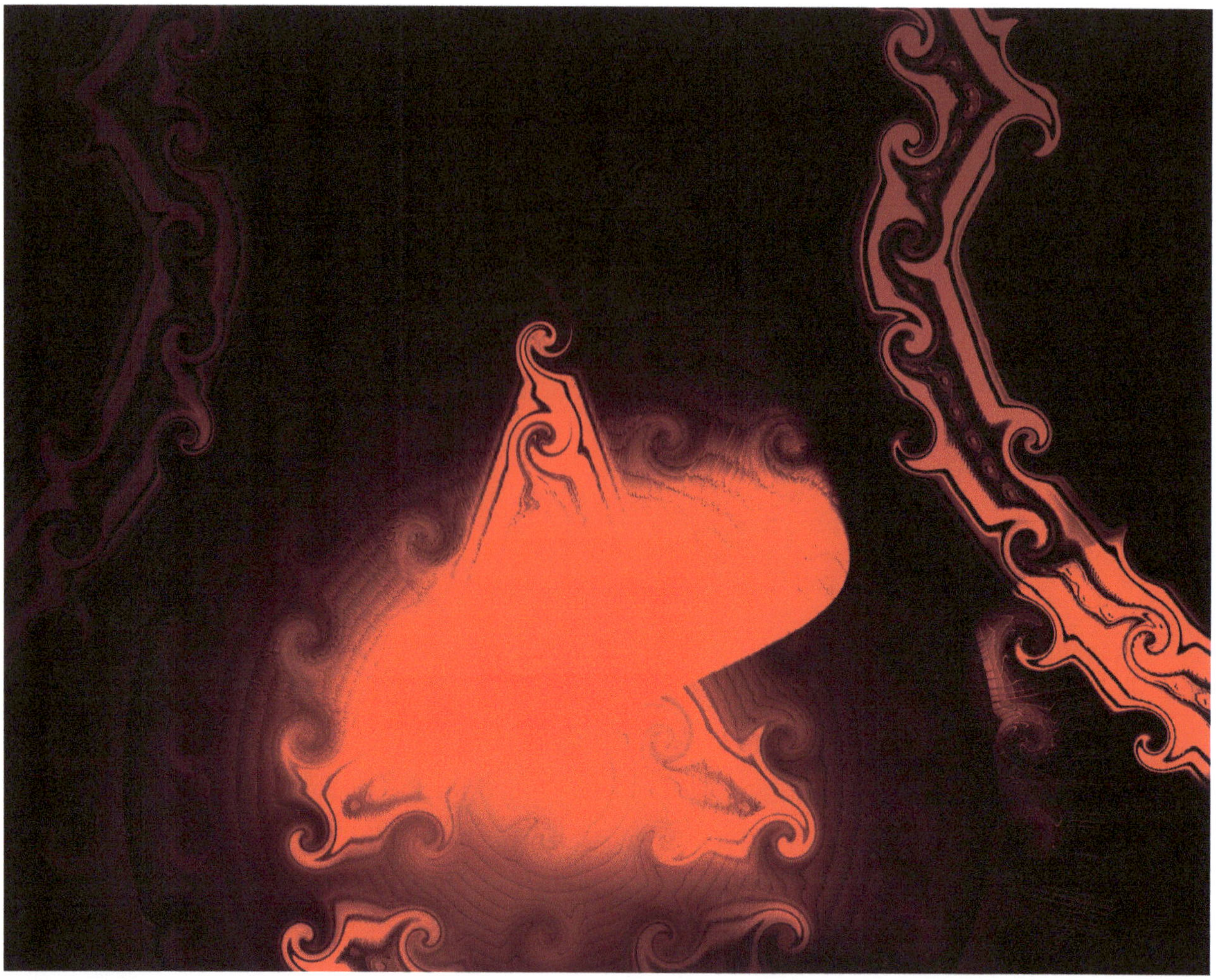

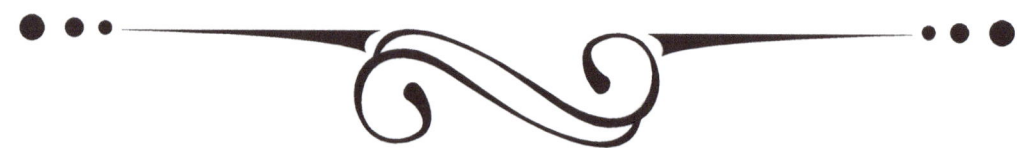

THE DESCENT OF MAN

The Descent of Man came to be given the duality of what the word decent can mean. I always add a bit of cryptic imagery to my abstracts maybe you can see them all.

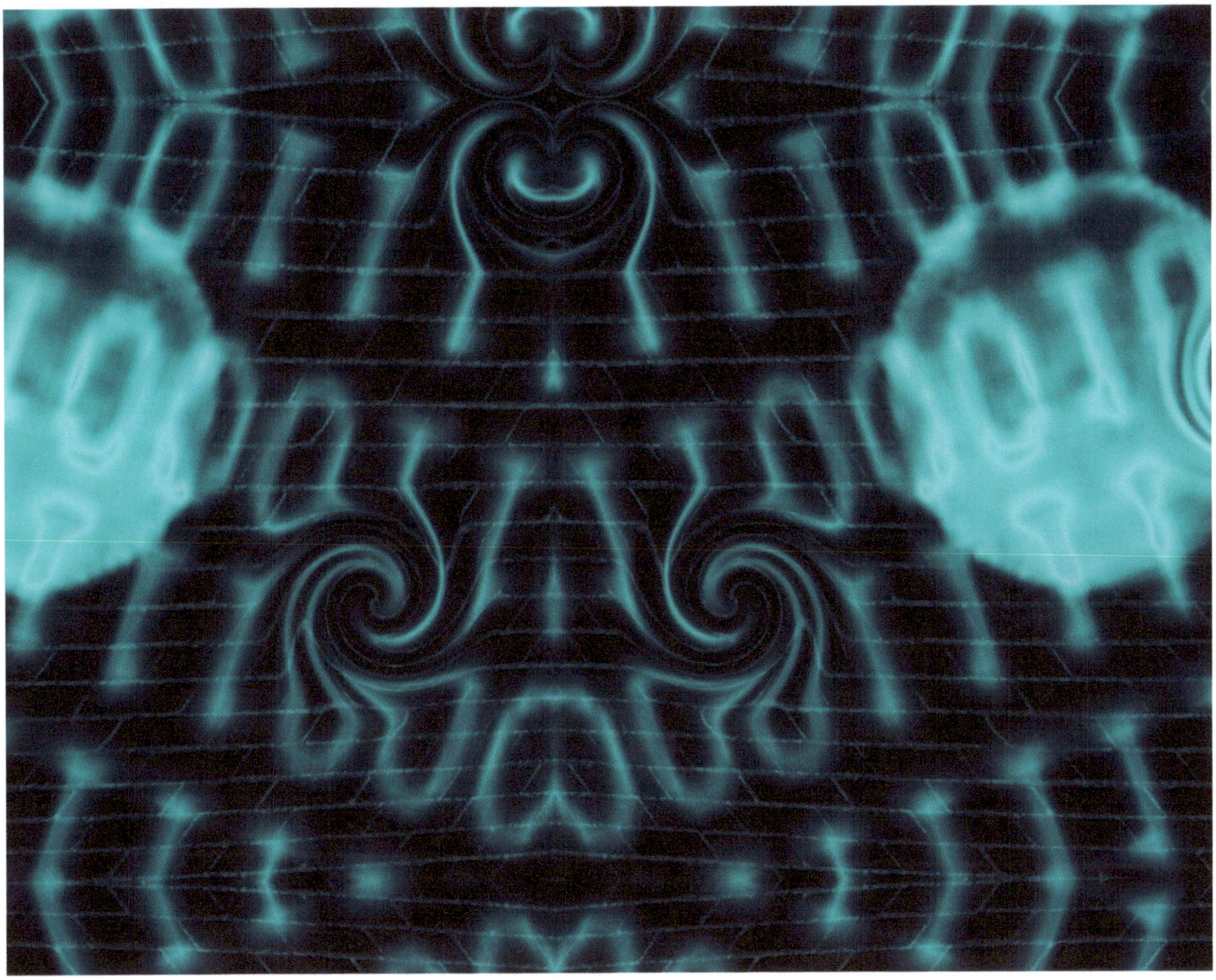

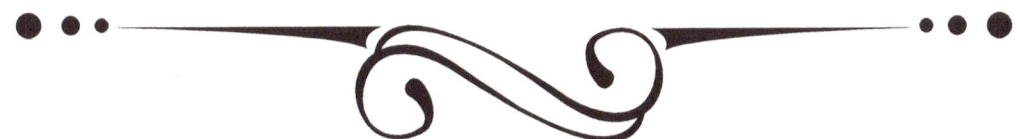

ETHOS

A Cryptic abstract that came to mind as personal thoughts of what the modern Ethos was to me. An urbanized world, reaching into the cyber world and out into the cosmos. When joined together, they create a new mythology.

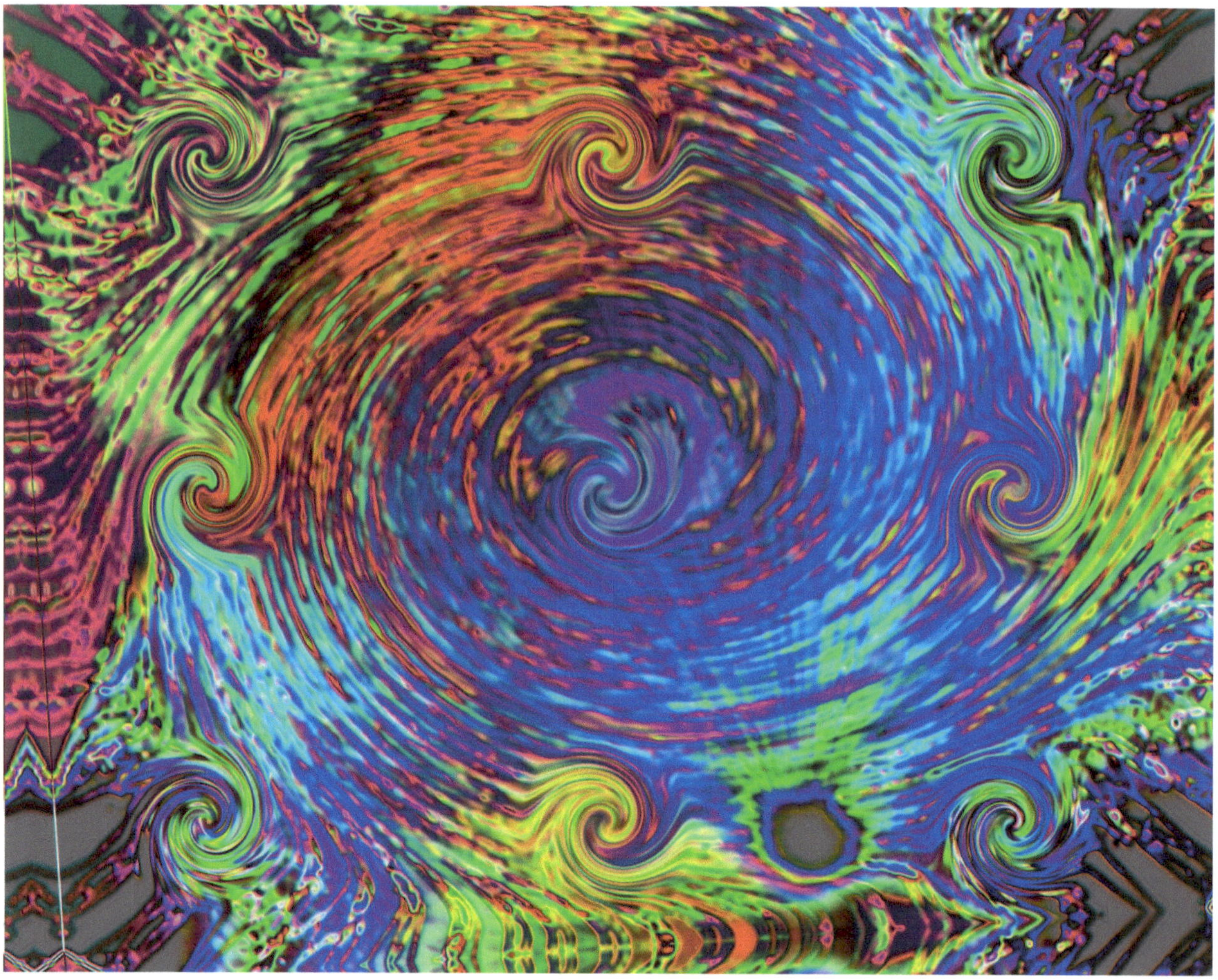

TYRANTS

The six senses become Tyrants to an open, observant mind. The world without filters such is the life of an artist.

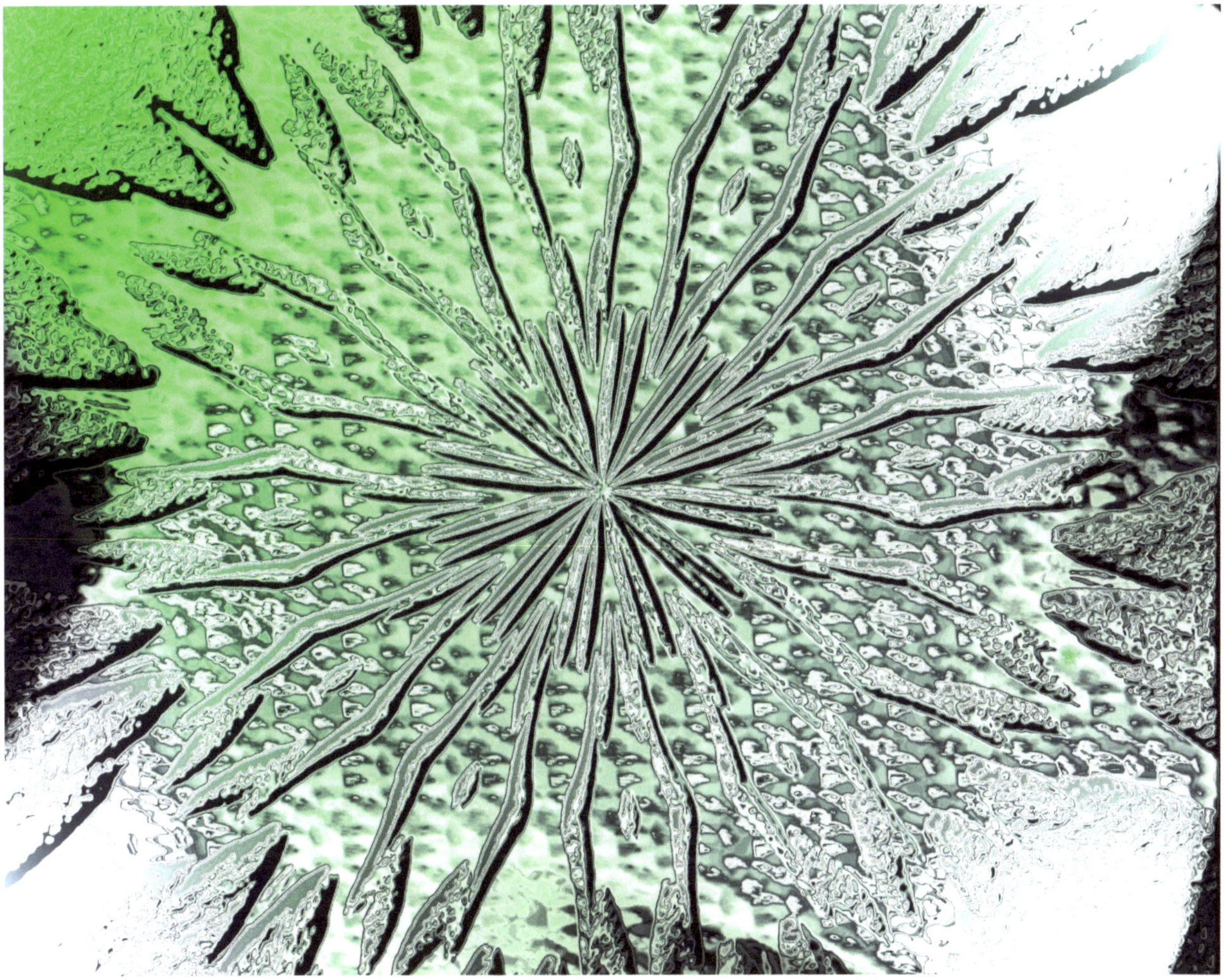

THE STRUGGLE

The struggle came to me as the seasons changed two different things that grow in different ways struggling to stay in existence.

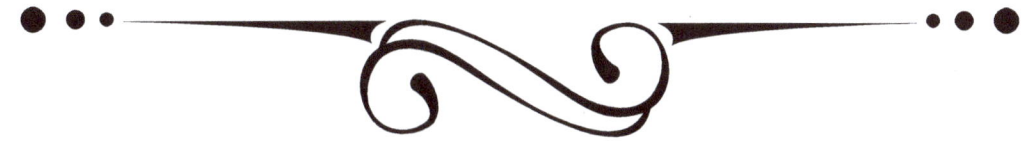

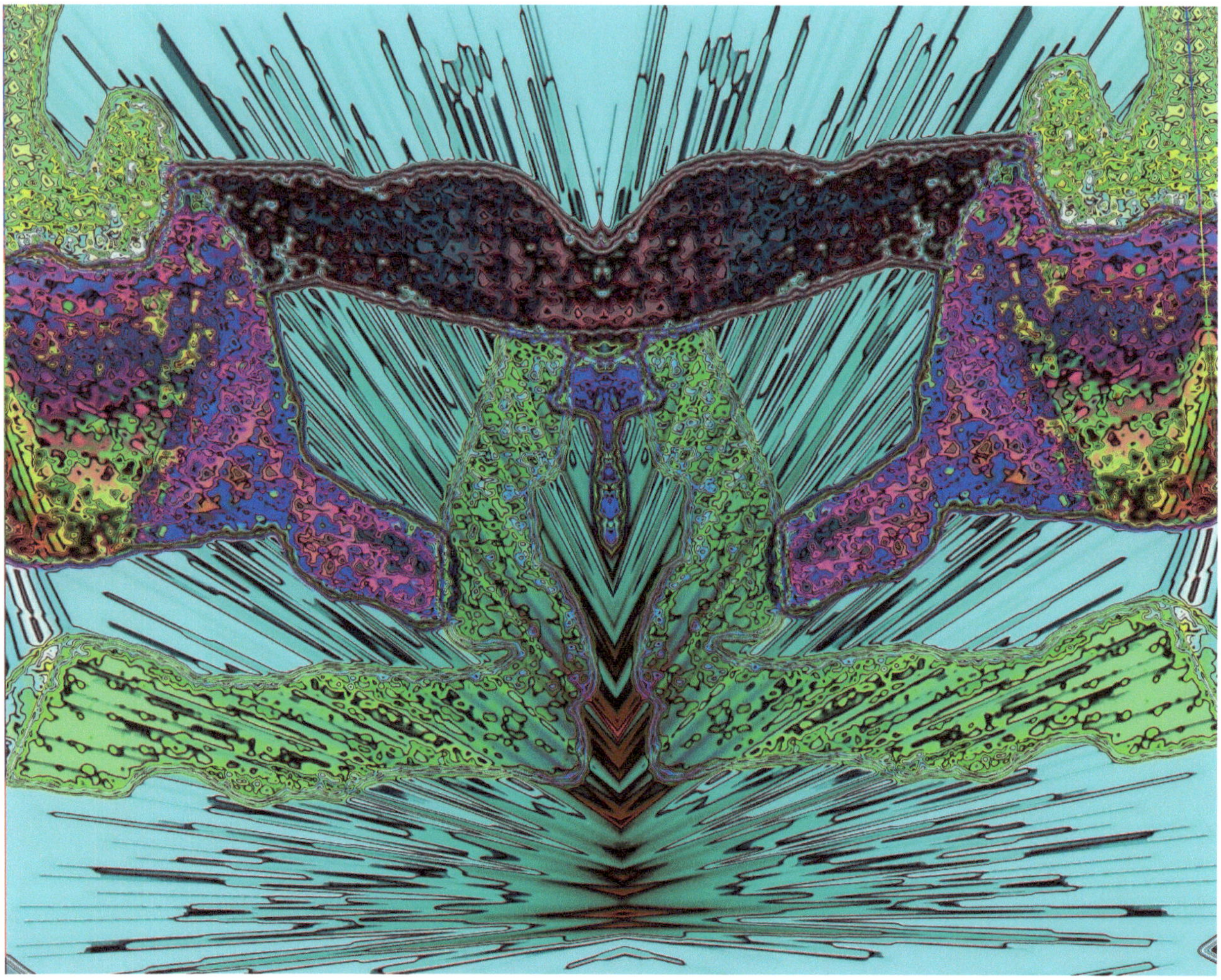

WE ARE WITH YOU

Sometimes when you work with abstracts, You start to see things that are not there. Such is how this work got the name "We are with you." I finished this work, and I looked deeply into it, and I saw many faces. It reminded me, each work of art I make is something I brought life, and they will always be with me.

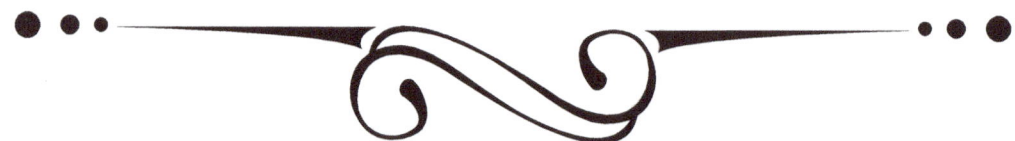

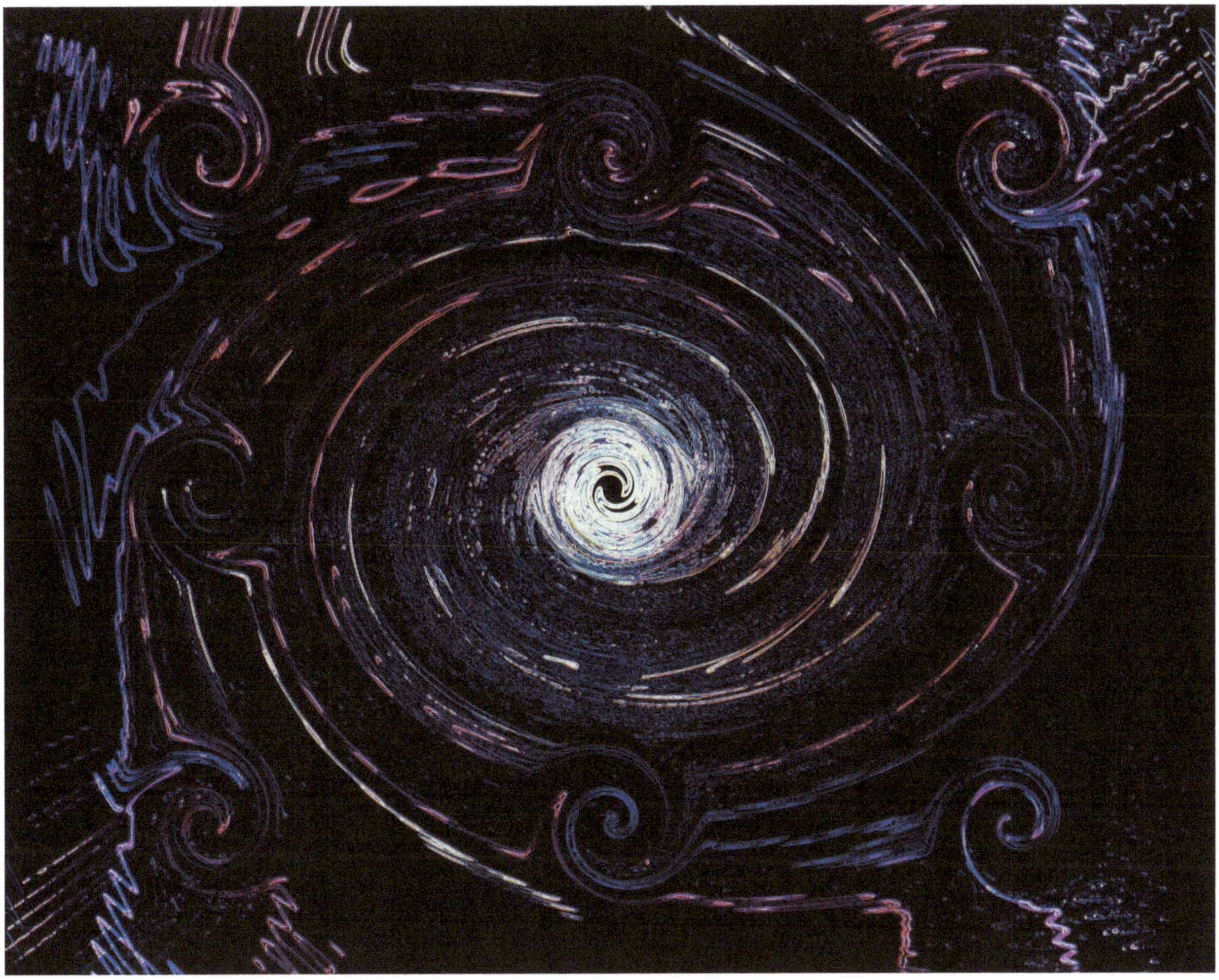

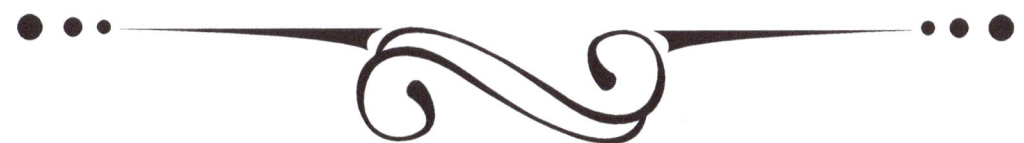

LOOKING IN OR LOOKING OUT

I was just coming to the realization of light is the first thing you see when you're born and often the last thing you see before you die, and it brought the question to mind are they indeed the same moment? Birth and rebirth with no end to the cycle of creation.

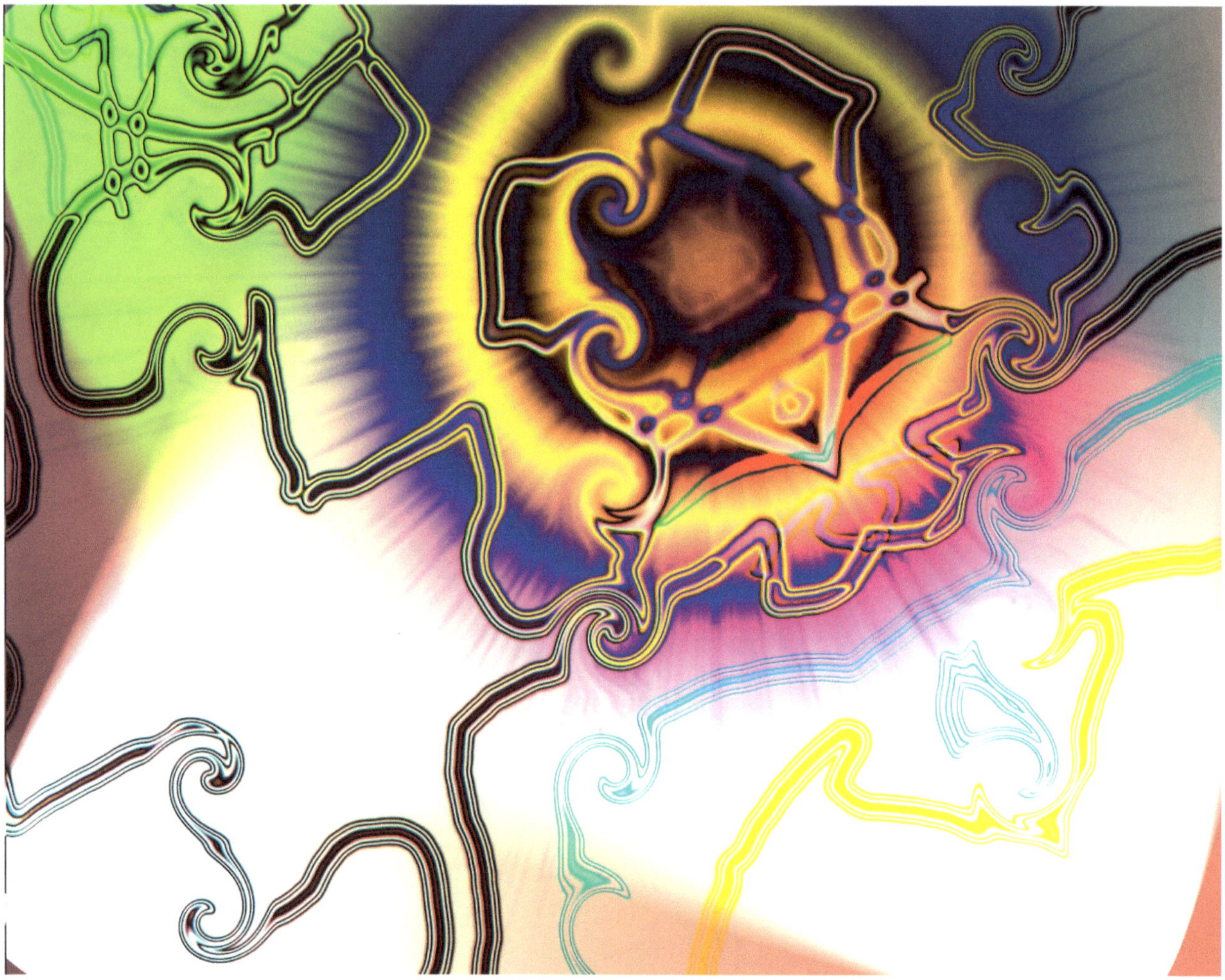

EROS

What is it to see the energy of Eros? The light, the dark, the fractured thought. To look into the center of it and see beyond the veil of human eyes. This is my vision of Eros.

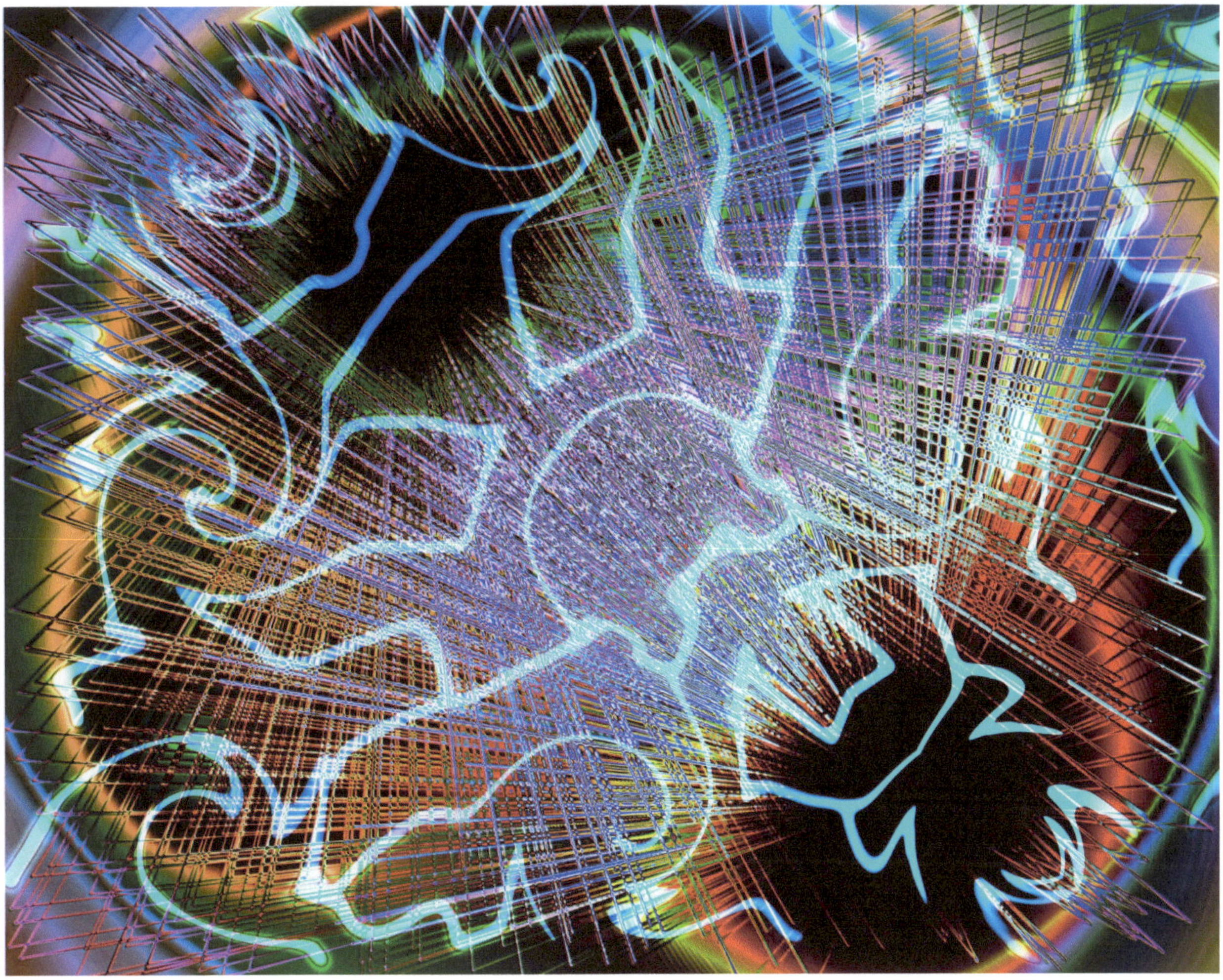

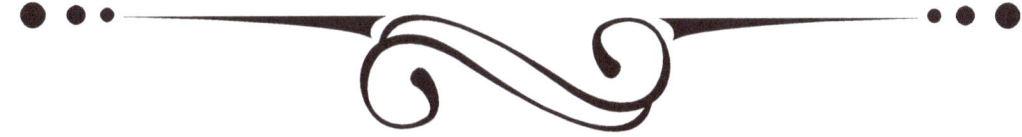

DEFIANT PRIDE

There are times when one must stand against authority in defiance and not waver with only your honor as your shield.

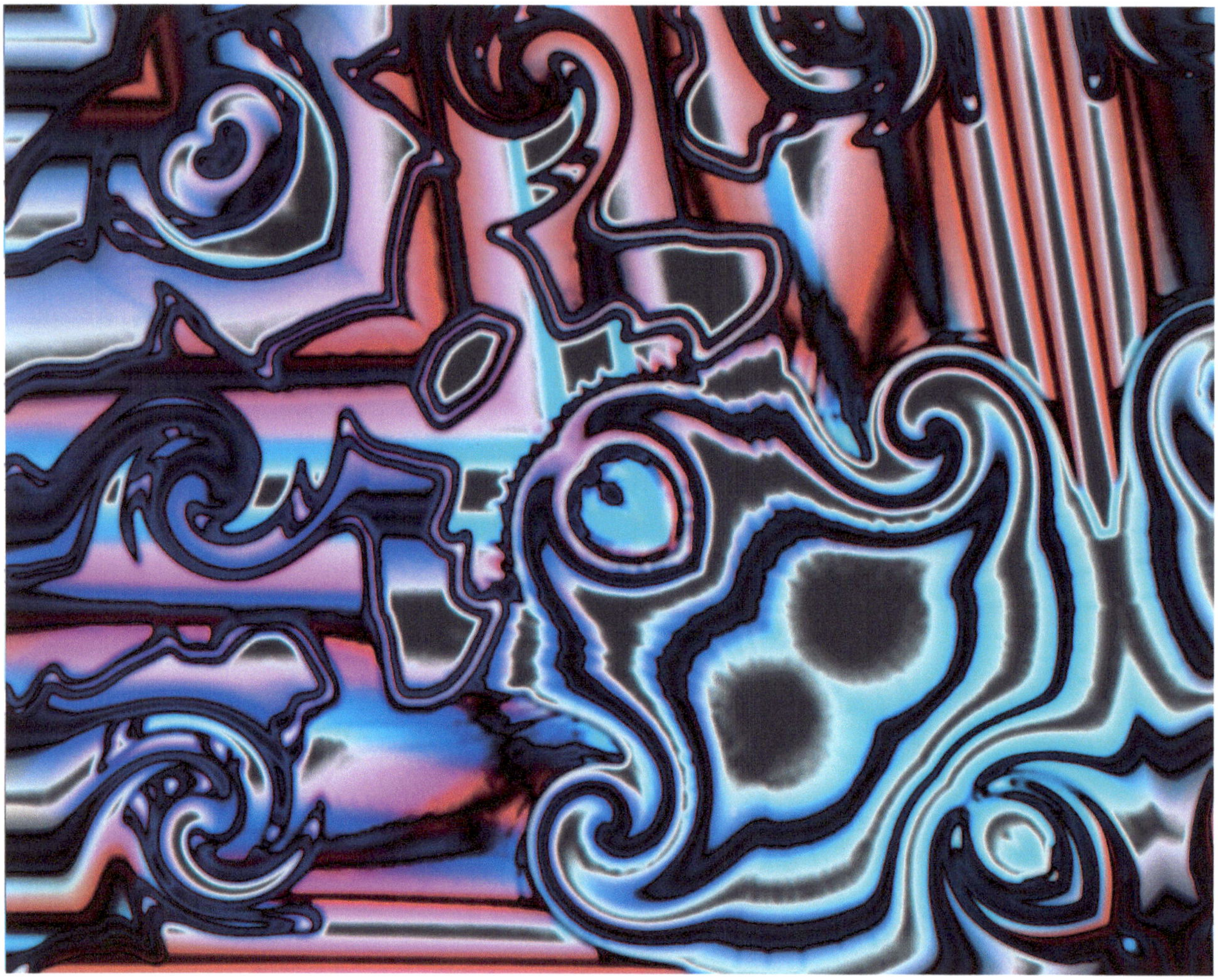

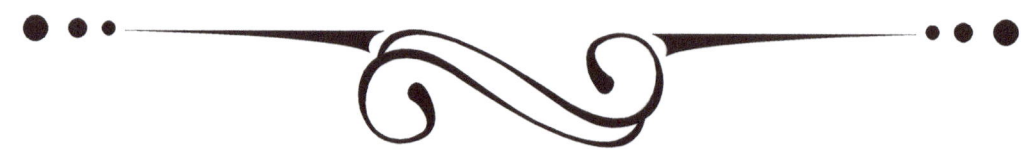

NEMESIS

There can be no reason, No diplomacy, Two adversaries set at odds in a never-ending circle. Even the greatest of prophets must acknowledge a difference in philosophy makes for the longest and hardest of wars.

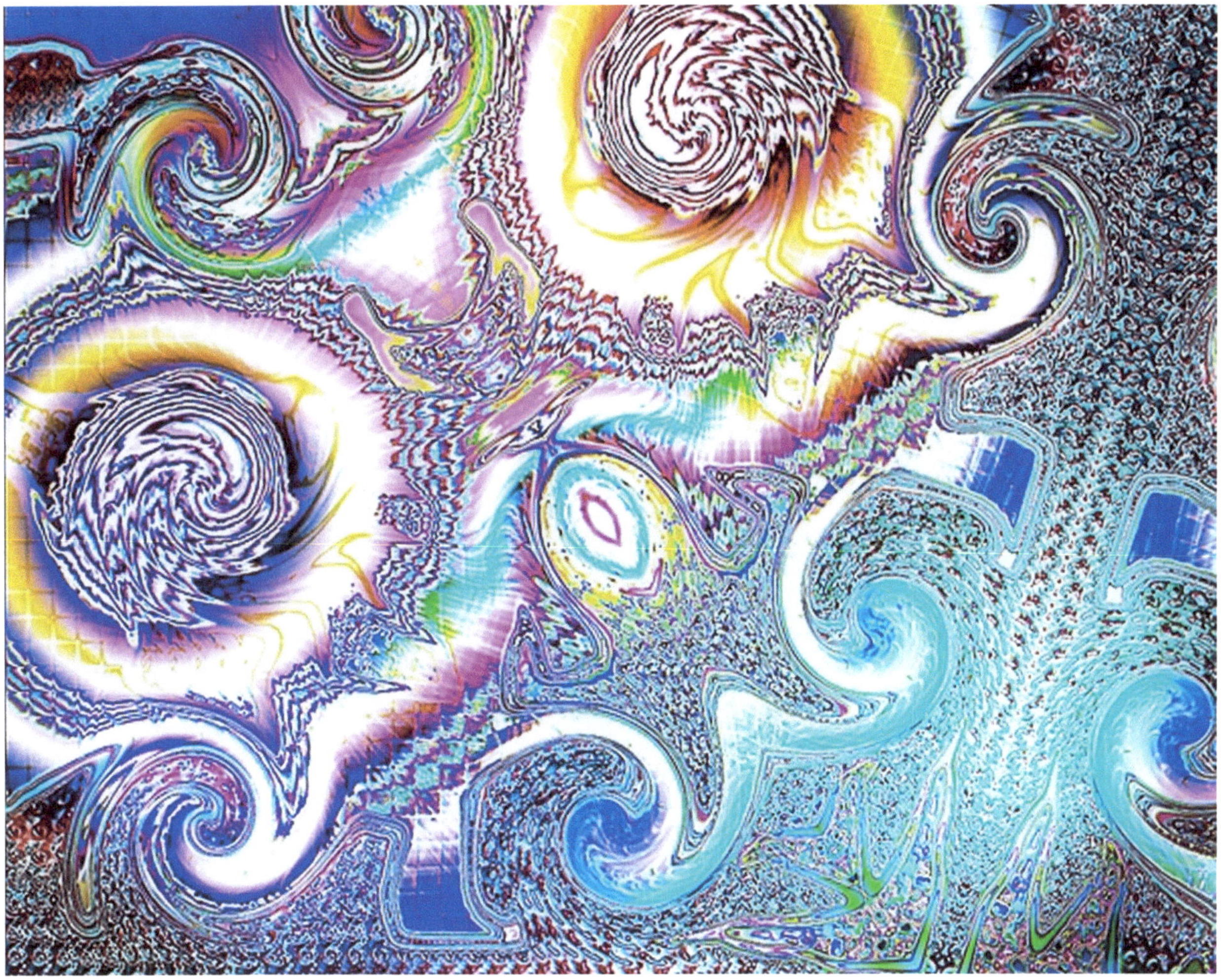

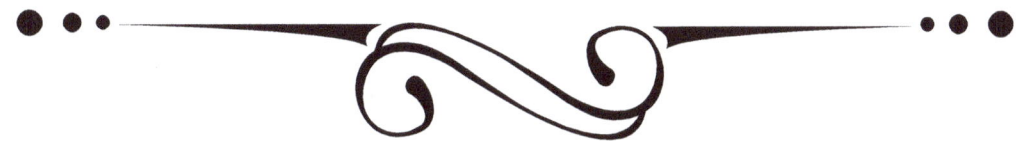

THE ESSENCE OF MAN

Light, aura, energy, and the sub-atomic. What is the essence of man? More than the mere matter we think, we see every day. Luminous beings we are and always will be when we start viewing the world through different eyes.

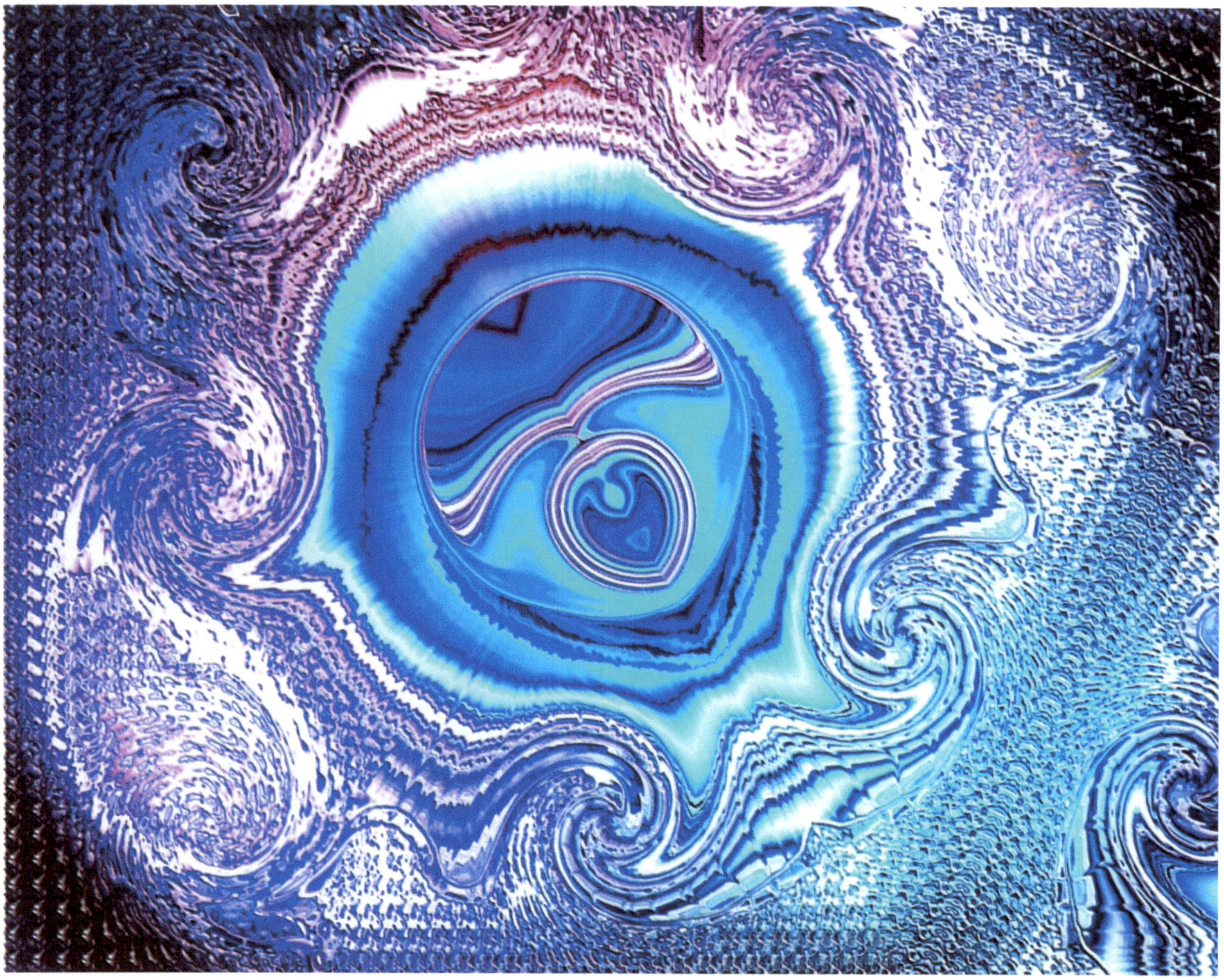

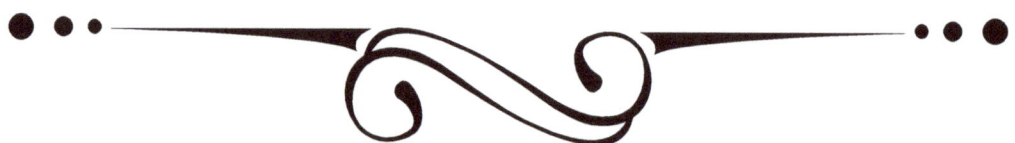

LOOKING PAST THE VEIL

Looking past the veil into unknown worlds, Viewing all yet disconnected. A stranger in a strange land. This is not only my sentiment when I look beyond but often in my own world. A person out of time and out of place.

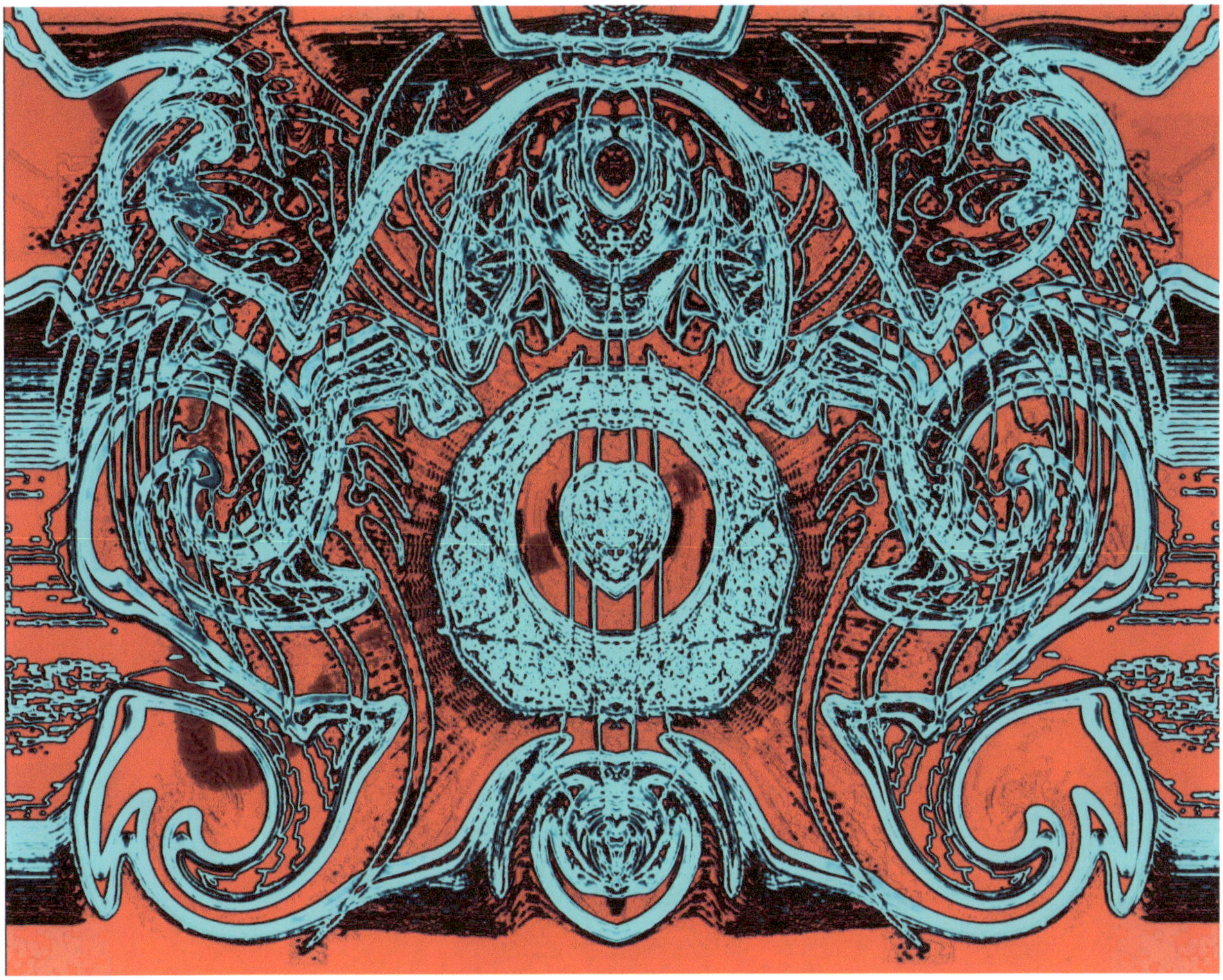

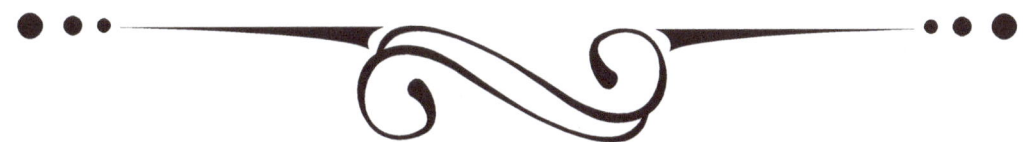

ILLUSIONS OF GOOD AND EVIL

Deep inside the soul, there is the capacity to be beautiful or hateful. Does one side rule, or is it all an illusions. The forces at work call to be looked upon not judged but accepted.

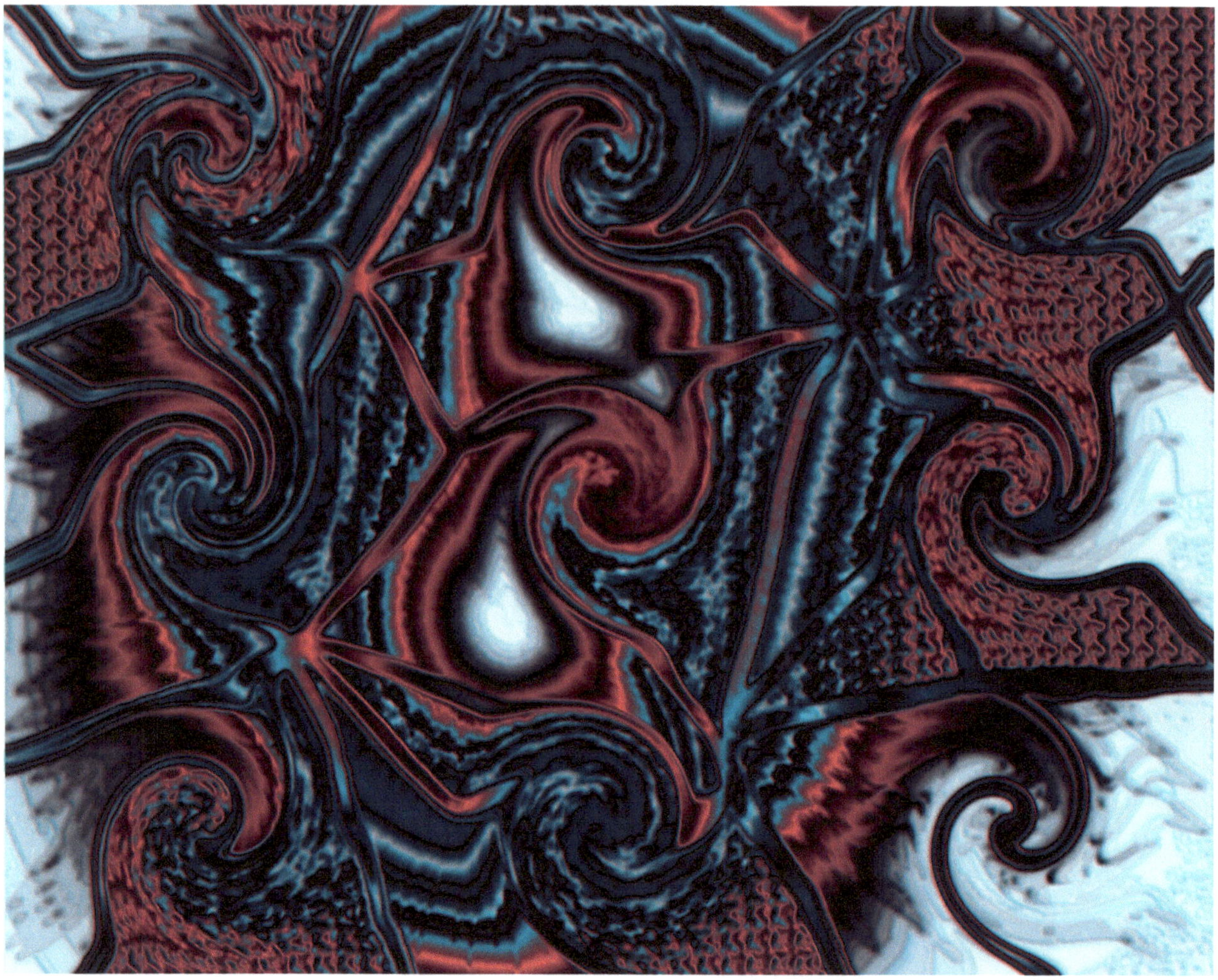

DECISIONS LOST SEED

One choice, one moment in time changes the outcome of what is and will before forever. Decisions lost seed a lock on the gateway of evolving time.

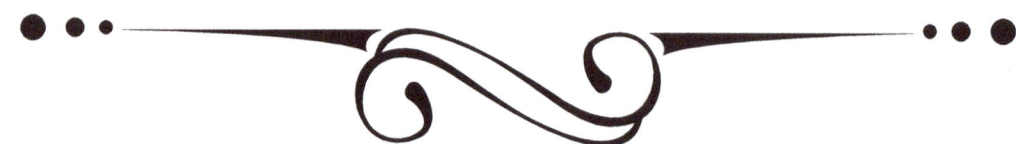

ABOUT MARK HUMES

Mark Humes is a Digital abstract artist, author, and the owner of Mark Humes Gallery. He continues to create works of art and art books to share his unique visions with the world. His artwork can be viewed at www.markhumes.gallery

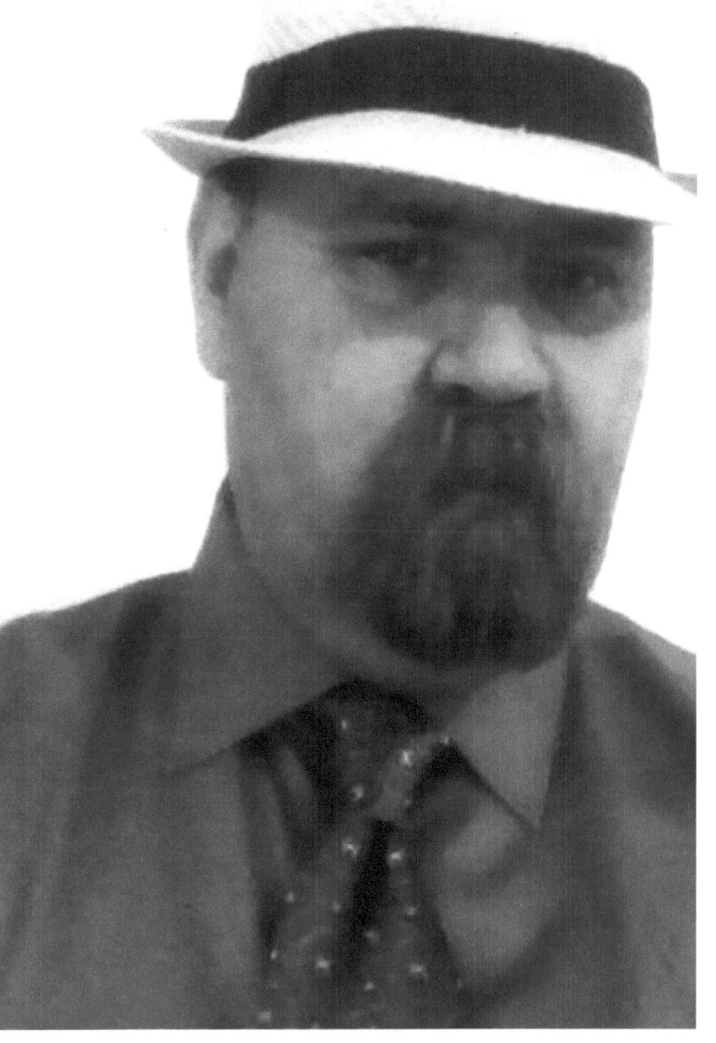

www.ingramcontent.com/pod-product-compliance
Lightning Source LLC
Chambersburg PA
CBHW040745200526
45159CB00023B/1731